The Land of Light
LYCIA

Archaeologist
İlhan Akşit

akşit

AKŞİT KÜLTÜR ve TURİZM TİCARET LTD. ŞTİ.

Table of Contents

Published by:

AKŞİT KÜLTÜR TURİZM SANAT AJANS LTD. ŞTİ.

To place orders, please contact:

Cağaloğlu Yokuşu Cemal Nadir Sokak Nur İş Hanı 2/4

34440 Cağaloğlu   İSTANBUL - TURKEY

Tel: (0212) 511 53 85 - 511 67. 82 Fax: (0212) 527 68 13

Author	: Archaeologist İlhan Akşit
Translator and	
Editor	: Stuart Kline
Photographers	: Güngör Özsoy, Kadir Kır, Erol Uziyel, Mustafa Salur, Tahsin Aydoğmuş
Graphics	: Bülent Sarı,
Color Separation	: Figür Grafik A.Ş.
Printing House	: Seçil Ofset Ltd. Şti.
Binding	: Çağ Cilt Sanayii A.Ş.

Preface

In ancient times, the region known today as the Teke Peninsula, which encompasses an area from the Dalaman Stream in the west all the way to Phaselis on the western outskirts of modern day Antalya, was called Lycia and the people living there were known as Lycians.

Throughout ancient history, the Lycians had always held a distinctive place among the various races of Anatolia. Locked away in their mountainous country, they had a fierce love of freedom and independence.

With its historical artifacts sheltered within, Lycia is practically an open-air museum and is Anatolia's most mysterious region, a place where green forests surround lacy coves and shade the deep blue water.

Just as many places that are found in the Lycian region are accessible over land as they are by boat. For instance, the Fethiye bays, as well as Kekova, which are full of historical artifacts, present blue voyagers with incomparable beauty.

In addition, just as those yachts arriving in Fethiye are able to cruise the bays in the Fethiye Gulf, boats dropping anchor off Kalkan or Kaş have the possibility to make day trips to any number of ancient cities such as Patara, Letoon and Xanthos. Thus, history becomes intertwined with the sea.

Driving around the Lycian region over roads shaded by pine trees is your other, quite pleasant, option.

Though we might not be able to date Lycian cities prior to the 7th century B.C., we know that Lycians joined the Hittites to fight in the Kadesh War, whereby Lycians under the command of King Sarpedon went to the assistance of the Trojans. Even if the ancient writer Herodotus had written that the Lycians had come from Crete, this is an incorrect statement. The latest evidence we have gathered from excavations carried out in the region is that these people known by the Hittites as 'Lukkas' were natives of Anatolia, that they had been living in this region for many years and that they called themselves 'Termilae'.

Pilinius the historian said that there were once 70 Lycian settlements in the region, but that by his time, this number had dropped to 36.

Our book, which starts from the western end of the region, will introduce to you all of the Lycian cities whose names and locations are definitively known. Whereas we shall try to present you a fascinating and detailed glimpse into the Lycian's thoroughly original civilization as well as their mysterious world.

I would also like to take this time to thank our American colleague, Mr. Stuart Kline for his fine translation and editing contributions.

Archaeologist

Ilhan Akşit

June 5th, 1998

Feneryolu, Istanbul

Lycia and the Lycians

"I have come a long way from here to help

I have come from distant Lycia and the eddying Xanthos,

where I settled my dear wife, child and enough business and personal effects

to make the poor and destitute salivate in anticipation.

Once again, I've taken the Lycians into battle

Look, and you will see me out in the very front"

These words were uttered by the leader of the Lycians, Sarpedon during the Trojan Wars to encourage to the Trojan Prince Hector. What we percieve from these words is that the Lycians, under the command of Sarpedon, had come to aid Troy during the Trojan Wars of the 12th century B.C. This means there were Lycians in the 12th century B.C. Sarpedon meant that he came from faraway Lycia, from the 'eddying Xanthos'. The Xanthos Stream is the ancient name of the Eşen Stream, which separates the provincial borders of modern day Muğla and Antalya. As is known, this stream took its name from the ruins of the ruins of Xanthos, which once lined its banks in splendor. Lycia may be roughly defined as the country lying within the Teke Peninsula, from Dalaman Stream in the west to Konyaaltı, just outside Antalya to the east. Fethiye, Kaş and Finike are all located within this region which, in ancient times was called Lycia and its people were called Lycians.

Where did these Lycians, who existed in the 12th century B.C., come from and since when had they been living in this land?

Evidence uncovered in archaeological digs in the Karataş-Semahöyük (Elmalı) has proven that the area was settled in the 3rd millennium B.C. An axe found in Tlos belongs to the year 2000 B.C. This indicates to us that there were settlements in the region in the 2nd millennium.

Chronologically, much surer ground is afforded by Hittite cunieform texts, which refer a number of times to a nation of the Lukka, whose language was called Luvian and who can be no other than the Lycians. Because, we learn for certain from the Iliad that they lived in this region in the last quarter of the 2nd millenium, that they were called Lycians and that they were ruled by a king named Sarpedon. In addition, the Hittite King Tudhalia IV (1250-1220 B.C.) was

A Colossal Sarcophagus Near Kale Village (Simena) (Luigy Mayer) London, 1804

An impressive sunset which was seen throughout the ages in the illuminated nation of Lycia.

known to have uttered, "I made sacrifices and presented gifts opposite Patar Mountain, I erected stelai, and constructed sacred buildings," which was a clear indication of Lycia's existence at that time. Thus, we understand that the people who called themselves *Trimilae* and whom we refer to as the Lycians, were the oldest tribe of Anatolia who lived without interruption in the Mediterranean Sea region.

Anatolia was never uninhabited, for every new arriving tribe would melt in their own crucible, give it shape, create a civilization on it, whereas these civilizations would pass through other countries or else influence them. For this reason, the artifacts and ancient cities seen in Anatolia were works created by these peoples, that is, the people of Anatolia.

Again, we see that the Lycians made it as far as Egypt by sea in 1227 B.C. Thus, it is revealed just how much the Lycians had mastered the seas during these years. In addition, we know that the Lycians were allied with the Hittites in their fight against the Egyptians during the Kadesh War which took place in 1295 B.C. As a result of a series of consecutive and uninterrupted attacks from sea tribes, the Hittite State was destroyed in the 12th century B.C. and in its place, the Phrygian State was established in Central Anatolia, in the vicinity of modern day Eskişehir and Kütahya. It was once commonly believed that the Phrygians did not spread as far south as the Lycian region, but evidence refuting this belief was recently uncovered at the latest diggings near Elmalı indicating that the Phrygians did spread out as far as the Lycian region.

Once the Phrygians were annihilated, the Lydian State was established in Western Anatolia. After they were defeated by the Persians in 546 B.C., the Persians reigned supreme over all of Anatolia. Lycia, which had never succumbed to Lydian rule, put up some major resistance against the Persians, who had arrived to take over their land.

Though the Xanthians put up a heroic fight, in which they were beaten by the superior Persian forces, and rather be captured as prisoners, the preferred to commit mass suicide;

"We had turned our homes into graves and graves our homes,

Our homes, destroyed, our graves plundered

We climbed the highest peaks and burrowed underground,

We remained underwater,

They came and found us, burned and destroyed us,

We, who have preferred mass suicide for the sake of our mothers, our women and our dead

We left behind a pyre of people to this earth, a pyre that doesn't burn out and won't do so in the future."

Thus, Lycia submitted to General Harpagus' superior Persian forces.

In 480 B.C., when the Persians assembled their huge force for the conquest of Greece, the Lycians contributed fifty ships to his fleet, which showed that they were a sea power to be reckoned with. Ancient historians state that the Persians never established complete sovereignty over the Lycians.

We know that Pisidians, Cilicians, Pamfilians and Lycians allied themselves with the dynasts to rebel against the Persians.

The Lycians, who went into action without

Lycian sarcophagus. Erected around 400 B.C., this sarcophagus carries the defined characteristics of sarcophagi in the Lycian region. It was found in Sidon and is now located in the Istanbul Archaeology Museum.

being dependent on any dynast, must have thought that perhaps they could eliminate the slack Persian rule. This rebellion was suppressed thanks to the Carian dynast Mausolus, who took advantage of this slack rule to extend his claims over the whole of Lycia. Lycia attempted an accord during the first half of the 4th century B.C., whereas the formation of this accord was ensured by the Limyran dynast Pericles.

Alexander the Great encountered a cordial welcome with practically no resistance from the Lycians upon his arrival on the scene in the winter of 333 B.C. It wasn't a matter of being afraid of Alexander, but rather because the Lycians were angry at the Persians who forced them under Carian sovereignty. In appointing one of his commanders, Nearkhos to govern here, Alexander continued on his journey, whereas Lycia ceased to be free. Because we see that Lycia's culture, which had not changed despite all the difficulties suffered up to then, had been transformed.

After the death of Alexander, Lycia passed under the rule of Antigonos, then in 310 B.C., by his general Ptolemy, who had established himself as king of Egypt. Later on, Lycia was ruled by Lysimakhos and finally was retaken by the Ptolemies in 296 B.C., who put an end to the Lycian language and replaced it with Greek whereas the cities also adopted Greek constitutions.

In 197 B.C., the country was taken from the Ptolemies by King Antiochus III, of Syria. Shortly afterwards, he was defeated by the Romans at the battle of Magnesia; whereas in the settlement which followed in 190 B.C., the Lycian region was given to the Rhodians, who had supported Rome. The Lycians, intolerant as ever of foreign domination, just couldn't accept the fact that they were put under Rhodian rule. Rather than obey the Rhodians, the Lycians rebelled in 187 B.C. but were not successful in this attempt. Another uprising took place six years later, whereby the Lycians sent a delegation to Rome stating that they were being treated like slaves and that their honor and dignity were at stake in this matter. The Senate gave the Lycians a favorable reply, to the effect that they were supposed to be merely friends and allies of the Rhodians. Encouraged by this, the Lycians took up arms again, and hostilities continued for another six years, but by 171 B.C., the Lycians were again exhausted. In the manwhile, Rome's relationship with Rhodes had cooled considerably, and consequently, the Senate decided to put an end to Rhodian control of Caria and Lycia and declared these countries free in 167 B.C.

23 cities joined the Lycian League which was established at this time. Of these, Tlos, Xanthos, Pınara, Patara, Myra and Olympos each had three votes. In addition, cities such as Antiphellos, Aperlae, Arycanda, Candyba, Cyaenai, Limyra, Phellos, Rhodiapolis, Sidyma, Telmessos, Araxa and Podalia were all members of this League and minted coins in their own names. This League had a Senate which held a congress every autumn to take care of the League's business and decide on issues such as war, peace, army organiation and budgetary matters. A Lyciarch, who would be chosen at these meetings, held this post for a period of one year.

Thus, while the Lycians were carrying out their lives through this League, King Attalos III of Bergama died in 133 B.C., whereby Rome gained possession of all Asia Minor lands. In 88 B.C., the King of Pontus, Mithridates attacked southern Asia Minor. Together with the Romans, the Lycians resisted the Pontus King. The war ended in 84 B.C. with the king's defeat by Sulla, and in the subsequent settlement the Romans showed how much they appreciated Lycian loyalty by confirming their freedom and expanding their lands to include the three northern cities of Bubon, Oenodanda and Balburo.

Cilician pirates had threatened the Mediterranean coastline in the Roman period. In 78 B.C. we see that the Lycian admiral Aechmon battled with the Romans against the pirate chief, Zenicetes, who was using Olympos as a base. After Zenicetes was beaten by the Romans, Lycia was spared of this trouble. However, both Olympos, which had offered the pirates sanctuary and Phaselis, which had played the accomplice, were expelled from the Chorikos League.

We see that the Lycians sided with Caesar in the Roman civil war between Caesar and Pompeius. Nevertheless, Caesar was assasinated in Rome, whereas Caesar's murderers, Brutus and Cassius, passed over to Asia Minor to collect money and soldiers. The Lycians were reluctant to make any contributions to Brutus' resources, which resulted in Romans attacking Xanthos, where the Lycian League's soldiers were gathered. Though the Lycians battled the opposing forces fiercely, they could not gain the upper hand, and consequenctly, Xanthos fell. For the second time in their history, the Xanthians underwent mass suicide for their freedom in the year 42 B.C.

After Brutus entered the fallen city, a woman was seen hanging from a noose with her dead child slung from her neck, whereby Brutus was moved to tears. He proclaimed a reward for any of his soldiers who saved a Lycian from destruction. Only about 150 Xanthians fell alive into Roman hands.

Later on, Roman armies took control of Lycia by beating Brutus and went about repairing the destroyed city. Antoninius, who defeated Brutus, took over Rome's eastern territories and gave the Lycians their freedom. As a consequence, Lycia remained the only part of Asia Minor not to be incorporated within Rome's sphere of power.

The Empire period, which began with Augustus, was one that witnessed the recovery and expansion of Lycia from every aspect. Some of the emperors passing through Lycia as well as wealthy local citizens transformed these lands with numerous public works projects.

Roman emperors Germanicus and Vespasian paid visits to Lycia in 17 B.C. and 69 A.D., respectively. In proclaiming the Xanthians as benefactors of the universe, Vespasian had a victory arch erected in his name. Finally, Emperor Trianus called on Lycia in 113 A.D. Thus, Lycia continued to prosper as a Roman province.

Lycia was devastated by a temblor that struck in 141 A.D., whereby both Rome and the rich local inhabitants attempted to compensate for the damage. However, another quake destroyed Lycia once more on August 5, 240 A.D. Subsequent to this earthquake, pirates sprouted up out of the woodwork, which caused the demise of some of the Lycian cities.

At this time, the boundary was extended to the northwest to include Caunus. While the struggle between Christianity and Paganism continued, we see that Christianity gradually spread throughout the region, whereas Myra become the region's metropolis. Lycian cities continued their existence into the Byzantine Age, however subsequent Arab raids, which started in the 8th century, were the reason for these cities to disappear one after another.

Lycian Tombs and Monuments

Throughout the ages in Anatolia, people have buried their dead using various burial rituals and have showed them respect in different manners. On occasion, they would incinerate the corpse and hide the ashes, sometimes the corpse would be interned in a large earthenware jar, whereas it is also known that they were buried in simple graves which did not have many characteristics.

In some ages, the graves were made into tumuli by piling soil on top of them, which turned them into distinctive and magnificent tombs. The most splendid of these tumulus tombs were Phrygian King Midas' 53 meter high tomb in Gordion as well as that of the Lydian King Alyettes, which is located in Bintepeler near Sard and stands 69 meters high.

In addition to these types of tombs, the custom of burying the dead in a tomb resembling a house began in the second half of the 3rd millennium B.C. and continued without pause until the end of the Age of the Roman Empire. Naturally, from an architectural standpoint, these formed into several tomb structures, the most common of which are seen in the Lycian region. It is literally an open-air museum with all the various types of tombs seen here. Like elsewhere, the early buildings found in this region have been over-laid by those of the Hellenistic and especially the Roman periods; but the Lycian tombs, for which the country is famous, are in many cases earlier than the time of Alexander, and are moreover frequently adorned with sculpture works. Many are still in excellent preservation.

These early tombs fall into four distinct classes, generally called pillar-tombs, temple-tombs, house-tombs and sarcophagi.

Temple tombs are not specifically Lycian, and differ little from those Caunus and other parts of Anatolia. They have simply the facade of a temple, with two columns in antis, usually in the Ionic order, an epistyle, and a pediment. A porch leads through by a door to the grave-chamber, a plain room with stone benches on which the dead were laid. The most splendid of these is located on the hillside above the ancient city of Fethiye. Carved into the stone in the 4th century B.C. is the name of Amyntas, son of Hermapias. The man in question is quite unknown.

House-tombs are in imitation of wooden houses, in one, two, or occasionally three stories; the square beam-ends are left projecting over the sides. Normally, there is a row of round or square beam-ends above the door; later these develop into a dentil frieze. There is sometimes, but not always, a pediment above, and in a few cases this has the shape of a pointed Gothic arch. These house-type tombs, which have a magical spellbinding effect on us, appear most frequently in Lycian cities such as Pınara, Tlos, Telmessos, Myra, Limyra, Antiphellos and Theimussa. House-

14

tombs are often decorated with reliefs on the walls, in the pediment, and sometimes on the adjoining rocks; a view of the city was carved into the stonework of a tomb in Pınara. The famous rock tombs of Myra are in two main groups. Just to the west of the theater the steep cliff is honeycombed with closely packed tombs of greatly varying form and size, though the majority are as usual of house-type. Many of these are quite elaborate, and some are decorated with reliefs in color. A few are of temple-type, others are extremely simple; sarcophagi are not in evidence. The second group of tombs is around the corner of the hill facing north-east, and is hardly less impressive than the other. This group of tombs should be visited before 10 o'clock in the morning in order to see them in the optimum light. Not very much above ground-level, and approached by a somewhat uncomfortable rock-path, is the monument known as the Painted Tomb, certainly one of the most striking in all Lycia. It is of the usual house-type and has in the interior a bench on the right and left sides; in front is a leveled platform with steps leading up to one side. But the outstanding feature is the group of eleven life-size painted figures in relief. The house-type stone tombs near the theater that have battle and feast scenes are situated in places that can easily be seen by those visiting Myra.

Besides these house-type tombs that were worked into the sheer rock face, there were also those that were made out of free-standing stone blocks. The finest examples representing this type are the tombs which are found to the west of the acropolis in Phellos, next to the theater in Xanthos as well as those behind the restaurants in Üçağız. Proceeding east from the landing-stage at Üçağız, one will see a pair of rock-cut house-type tombs located just behind the shore, the doors of which are broken wide open. To the immediate right is a standing figure of a young man or boy, and above the door is a Lycian inscription naming the owner as Kluwanimi. A sarcophagus in the amphitheater in Kaş dating back to the 4th century B.C. with belly dancers in bas-relief and women figurines on the inside as well as a tomb-house sarcophagus found in Cadyanda known as the Salas Monument also represent fine examples. The Salas Monument was erected in the 4th century B.C. by the Lycian Prince Salas for his wife, who was a Carian princess.

Besides house-type tombs, there are also monument tombs. The nicest example of these is the well-known Nereid Monument in Xanthos, named for the sculptures that were found among the columns, and which is an exceptionally richly decorated tomb dating to the 5th century B.C.

Temple-shaped Lycian tombs located in Caunus on the western Lycian border. (4 th century B.C.)

Only some of the architectural members remain, all the sculptures having been taken to the British Museum by the Englishman Sir Charles Fellows in 1840 where they are currently on display in the Lycia Room.

With their magnificent structure, tombs in the form of heroums, which were constructed to commemorate the heroes in the region, are striking to the eye. Unfortunately, the reliefs from the heroum known as the Gölbaşı Monument, which was discovered in Trysa, were taken from the enormous sarcophagus there and put on display in the Museum of Art History in Vienna. The wall, about 3 meters high, was covered on its inner face on all four side of the enclosure, and on its outer face on the south side, with a frieze in two horizontal bands representing scenes from mythology. Among these are episodes from 'The Iliad and the Odyssey,' from the exploits of Theseus, from the Seven against Thebes, battles of Greeks and Amazons and of Centaurs and Lapithae, as well as many other figures of doubtful attribution. As for the second heroum, it is one which was dedicated to King Pericles of Limyra and is currently under restoration. Friezes belonging to this monument were decorated with Caryatids and were also shipped to Austria.

Another type of tomb which we encounter in the region is that of the pillar-tomb and are usually reckoned to be the earliest and can be seen in Isinda, Cyaenai and in several other Lycian cities, as well. They consist of a rectangular pillar set on a base, with a grave-chamber at the top surmounted by a wide cap-stone. This is the least common type and seems to be confined to the western part of the country. There are six pillar-tombs next to the other tombs in the ancient city of Apollonia. On pillar-tombs, sculpture is confined, when it occurs at all, to the sides of the grave-chamber at the top; the well-

A view of the western necropolis of Myra, which is the finest example of 4th century B.C. house-type Lycian tombs.

known example is the so-called 'Harpy Tomb' in Xanthos, which dates back to 480 B.C. The massive base of which was cleared by excavators about 25 years ago; the pillar itself, with the grave-chamber and crowning slabs, stands 8 meters high. Large square lifting-bosses have been left projecting on three sides. The chamber at the top was of marble and decorated with reliefs depicting the Sirens carrying the souls of the dead, in the form of children, to the Isle of the Blessed. These were removed by Sir Charles Fellows and sent to the British Museum, whereas the covering stones were propped up by wooden struts and a pile of stones. The tomb remained in a mutilated state until 1957, when the Turkish authorities installed the cement casts which have done much to restore the beauty of the monument.

There is another monument, just to the south of the Harpy Tomb, which is also sepulchral but of a totally different type. It consists in fact of two tombs, a sarcophagus of normal Lycian type standing on a stunted pillar-tomb. In addition to these, there is a pillar-tomb in excellent preservation belonging to the 4th century B.C. and situated near the east foot of Xanthos' Roman acropolis hill. Its grave-chamber at the top is of white marble, without decoration.

Sarcophagi are of course one of the most common forms of tomb all over the world, but the early Lycian type is distinctive. It is generally remarkable for its height, and is in three parts, a base, a grave-chamber, and a crested 'Gothic' lid. The base is commonly used as a second grave-chamber (hyposorium), destined for the owner's slaves or dependents. Sarcophagi are also very frequently ornamented with reliefs, mostly on the sides and crest of the lid, but also in some cases on

This 4th century B.C. Lycian tomb situated in Xanthos represents one of the finest examples of pillar tombs.

the grave-chamber itself. In the Roman period, the sarcophagi become much smaller and simpler, whereas the lid is rounded, though still with a crest. Some of these were decorated with Medusa heads, Eros figures or wreaths, whereas rich reliefs depicting hunting, feasts and war scenes can be seen on sarcophagi of the Lycian period.

Though it was not found in the Lycian region, the sarcophagus that was uncovered in Sidon and is currently stored in the Istanbul Archaeology Museum, represents a fine example of this type.A great number of the sarcophagi with reliefs found in Lycia were taken abroad, whereas there remains only 18 examples in their original settings. One of the most important sarcophagi that was smuggled abroad, that with the 'Dereimis and Aischylos' reliefs, was found in Trysa and dates back to 380 B.C. It is currently in the Vienna Art Museum.

Erected in 360 B.C., little remains of the Payava sarcophagus, one of the finest at Xanthos as the splendid reliefs depicting four horses pulling a chariot on its lid and war scenes on its base have all long since been removed to London. Also displayed in the British Museum is the Merehi Sarcophagus, which dates from 390 B.C. and depicts war scenes on it as well. A sarcophagus, which was found in Trysa belonging to the Hellenistic Period with reliefs on it, has managed to remain in our country and can be found in the Istanbul Museum of Archaeology.

Sarcophagi such as the one in Xanthos with a fine relief of two lions mauling a bull, as well as another that has belly dancers and dates to the 4th century B.C. are classified under the 'relief-sarcophagus' group. A particularly fine specimen of this group, perhaps the finest in all Lycia, which

A 4th century B.C. Lycian sarcophagus which is located in Xanthos.

dates to 340 B.C and stands beside the municipal building in modern day Fethiye. It is one of the few sarcophagi with reliefs that has managed to stay in our country. A hundred years ago it was standing in the sea; the water-level, after rising since antiquity, has evidently fallen in recent times. Along with the sarcophagus found in Phellos, the Izrara monument and stone tombs with reliefs in Tlos, the Hoyran monument in village of Kapaklı, the Catabura sarcophagus in Limyra as well as the sarcophagus which sits in the middle of an avenue in Kaş are all the most captivating works that have survived to the present.

Most of the approximately 2,000 sarcophagi in the region belong to the Roman Age. One can see these Roman period sarcophagi in large groups in a number of Lycian cities such as Phaselis, Sidyma, Apollonia, Cyaenai, Sura, Isinda and Istlada as well as the necropolis located at the entrance of Patara.

Of course, it is impossible not to be saddened for the pieces that have already been smuggled out of the country. If anything, it should be our national duty to become more accountable for the precious few works that remain and ensure that they are not further damaged in the future.

Fethiye (Telmessos)

Situated on the slopes of Mendos Mountain, Fethiye was established on top of ancient Telmessos on the shore of Fethiye Gulf. For this reason, the majority of the ruins have remained under this quaint district. Because of the abundance of accommodation facilities, captivatingly beautiful coves and significant development in yacht tourism in recent years, Fethiye represents the center of excursion in the Western Lycian region. Fethiye, which is located 50 kilometers from Dalaman Airport, can be reached by highway from Muğla, Denizli and Antalya and can also be reached by sea. Those staying in Fethiye, which is chock full of history, nature and sea, can easily wander out to the ancient cities in the vicinity, such as Cadyanda, Pınara, Tlos, Sidyma, Xanthos, Letoon and Patara. Here, the temperature does not go below 16° C, and one can frolic in the surf for up to nine months a year.

The town, which gets its name from Telmessos, the son of the god Apollo, was captured by the Persian King, Harpagos and was annexed to the Carian Satrap. In the 5th century in the tribute-lists of the Delian Confederacy, Telmessos and the Lycians are listed separately; and in the 4th century we find the Lycians under their dynast Pericles fighting against the Telmessians, besieging them and reducing them to terms. The result of this may have been that Telmessos was then brought into Lycia, since the geographer who passes under the name of Scylax, writing in the same century, reckons the city as Lycian.

When Alexander arrived in the winter of 334-333 B.C., he made a peace agreement with the Telmessians, who readily joined him. Not long afterwards, however, Nearchus the Cretan, one of his trusted 'Companions' whom he had appointed satrap of the region, was obliged to recapture the city from a certain Antipatrides, who had gained control of it. The two men were old friends, and Nearchus asked permission to leave in the city a number of captive women singers and boys that he had with him. When this was granted, he gave the women's musical instruments to the boys to carry, with daggers concealed in the flute-cases; when the party was inside the citadel, the prisoners' escort took out the weapons and so seized the acropolis. This is described by the historian as a stratagem; others might call it sharp practice.

In 240 B.C., Telmessos was presented by Ptolemy III to another Ptolemy, son of Lysimachus; and at the settlement in 189 B.C. after the battle of Magnesia; it was given by the Romans to Eumenes of

The symbol of Fethiye is the tomb of Amynthas, son of Hermapias (4th century B.C.).

A panoramic view of Fethiye.

A view of Fethiye at night.

Pergamum, but 'the lands which had belonged to Ptolemy' were allowed to remain in his hands. So far as we know, Telmessos continued in the Pergamene Kingdom until that came to an end in 133 B.C.; it would then naturally be included in the Roman province of Asia. In 88 B.C., we hear that the Rhodians received help 'from the Telmessians and from the Lycians', implying that the city was not then included in Lycia. Later, certainly under the Empire and perhaps earlier, Telmessos was a normal member of the Lycian League. After the Mithridates wars, Telmessos was given to Rhodes. Like the other Lycian cities during this period, Telmessos also complained about Rhodian administration, and subsequently Rome retook Lycia back from Rhodes.

The city, which continued its existence into the Byzantine era, had lost its significance with the Arabian raids which occurred after the 7th century. In the 8th century, the city's name was changed to Anastasiupolis in honor of the Byzantine Emperor Anastasius II; by the following century this too gave way to the name Makri, which meant 'far city'. Later on, the city was called Megri, whereas Megri was finally changed to today's Fethiye in 1934, to commemorate the first Turkish pilot, Fethi Bey.

C. Texier, who saw Telmessos in the 1850's, indicated that the Apollo Temple and theater could be

The picturesque view of Fethiye Harbor.

seen at that time. Subsequent to C. Texier's visit, a major earthquake struck in 1856, which knocked down these structures, and when Fethiye was hit with a second devastating quake just over one hundred years later, in 1957, these ruins were completely destroyed. Today's Fethiye is what was built up after this second temblor more than forty years ago. Today, the theater, which was found near the quay of new Fethiye, has been uncovered. This theater, which was built in the Early Roman period and was renovated in the 2nd century A.D., had the capacity to hold 5,000 people.

A medieval castle situated on the acropolis hill, where the city was first established, is surrounded by a wall. Today, one can see the bottom portion of the wall, which was erected by Rome as well as the upper part, which was constructed during the Middle Ages. Whereas, the Rhodian Knights used this castle as well as Şövalye Island, located in the harbor, to hold the city under their control.

The Tomb of Amyntas, which is the most splendid and best known of all the tombs, is located on the east face of the city's acropolis and has become the symbol of Fethiye. Seen from the plain below, it gives a great impression of size from up close. It is of the temple-type, in the Ionic order. Four steps lead up to the porch with two columns between pilasters; halfway up the left-hand pilaster is inscribed, in letters of the 4th century B.C., the name of Amyntas, son of Hermapias. C. Texier, who saw this tomb in the 1850's, apparently wished to document the fact that he saw it as he signed the left upper corner of the grave door.

In the cliff-face further to the left are numerous other tombs; two of these are temple-tombs similar to that of Amyntas, and little less impressive. There are also a number of Lycian-type sarcophagi within the city. One of these is situated on the street directly below these stone monuments, while the other stands besides the municipal building near the quay. The

sarcophagus next to the municipal building is one of the few sarcophagi with reliefs that has managed to remain intact to the present. Both sides of the lid and of the surmounting crest carry reliefs showing rows of warriors with shields in their hands, with a man sitting in an armchair wearing long clothing on the right side. The ends of the lid are divided into four panels. This sarcophagus, which was erected around 340 B.C., used to have reliefs on the bottom part as well, which is understood from the drawings of both Sir Charles Fellows and C. Texier. In addition, there are two sarcophagi from the 4th century that are located in the Cumhuriyet District, one of which has reliefs. However, these reliefs are in poor condition.

The area around Fethiye is filled with many ancient cities. For instance, to the north-west of the Eşen Stream, about 45 kilometers outside Fethiye, lie the Pınara ruins in the village of Minare, which have some interesting Lycian rock tombs. Here ancient structures, such as the theater, odeion and temple are practically all intact. Again, in the ruins of Sidyma, which are found in the village of Dodurga to the south of Eşen Stream, are some tomb monuments worth seeing. One should also pay a visit to the ancient city of Tlos, which can be found in the village of Yaka about 40 kilometers outside Fethiye. Tlos, which was one of the six major Lycian cities, offers a striking view with its theater, baths, agora and stadium.

Arsada lies somewhat back from, and high above, the Xanthos Valley, on an upland plain on the side of Akdağ, the ancient Mt. Massicytus at an altitude of almost 1,000 meters. Arsada is not mentioned by any author in antiquity, but the identity is proved by an honorific decree of the Arsadans found on the spot, and by the evident survival of the name in the nearby village of Arsaköy. Of the town itself, none of the buildings remain, but in and around the village are a number of Lycian tombs, mostly of the 'Gothic' sarcophagus type, with at least one house-type rock tomb. Araxa is situated by the village of Ören at the upper, northern end of the Xanthos Valley, close under

Temple- and house-type monument tombs from the 4th century B.C. They are both situated above Fethiye.

28

the mountains. Not much now survives of Araxa, but down by the riverside lie numerous 'Gothic' sarcophagus lids with illegible inscriptions. But the most interesting tombs are in a group of a dozen cut into the rock at the base of a low hillock by the roadside about a kilometer and a half west of the village. Set on a high rounded hill steep on all sides but the south, remains of the ancient city of Oenoanda can be reached through the village of Incealiler, near Seki. The summit was occupied by a building now in ruins, and a number of cisterns or reservoirs; the public buildings stood on a succession of terraces descending gradually southwards. Northernmost and highest of these is the theater, a little over 30 meters in diameter. Oenoanda's chief claim to fame lies no doubt in the famous inscription by the Epicurean philosopher Diogenes. In addition, tombs at Oenoanda are many and various.

Just like today, people hundreds of years ago liked this beautiful region and settled in it. There are also some ancient settlements within the Fethiye Gulf. Among them are Krya, above Bedri Rahmi Cove; Lissa and Lydai, above Manastır Cove and the ancient city of Daidala in Inlice, on the way to Göcek.

The fabulous coves can be explored in Fethiye, which is complimented by nature and history. There is a natural beach that stretches 4 kilometers long, as well as those of Çalış and Karagözler, within the city limits. Just as one can enter the sea around here, one can also take a daily excursion boat ride to check out the Fethiye coves. This 12-island excursion is like a dream. In addition, Günlük, which is 19 kilometers away, Küçük Kargı, famous for its trees, Katrancı Cove, which is 17 kilometers away from Ölü Deniz and Kıdrak, which is 3 kilometers away from Belcekiz, is an ideal place to relax with its refreshing sea and dense pine forest. Also, Butterfly Valley, which is situated amongst the mountains 5-6 kilometers away from Ölü Deniz about 350 meters high, possesses unique beauty.

A view of Boynuz Bükü, one of the beautiful coves of Göcek.

As for Ölü Deniz, that is a excursion route of its own. The stone houses of nearby Kayaköy, which was a large city up to the year 1925, were emptied of its Greek inhabitants after the establishment of the Turkish Republic when they returned to their homeland. Modern accommodation facilities and a shopping center have been built in Hisarönü, which is seen on the way to Kayaköy.

An aerial view of Ölü Deniz.

In addition, there are enough remains on both Gemili Island and Karacaören Island which prove just how important they were in days of antiquity.

One can visit the museum in the center of the administrative district. Those who have had enough of the heat should head 50 kilometers outside of Fethiye for world-famous Saklı Kent Canyon, an 18-kilometer long trek of spectacular natural beauty. If that's not enough, then go on up to the Fethiye plateaus or even Yaka Park near Tlos to cool off. For sports lovers, one can parachute off Babadağ Mountain overlooking Ölü Deniz, go scuba diving 12 months a year, or even paddle a raft or canoe down either Dalaman or Eşen Streams. Fethiye is one of those rare spots where history and nature come together in a splendid way.

Ölü Deniz

Ölü Deniz is situated 17 kilometers from Fethiye and is famous for its splendid coves as well as its history. Once you come from Fethiye and pass through Hisarönü, which has become an entertainment and shopping center in recent years, you will encounter Ölü Deniz' myriad of blue hues with all the beauty of the splendid hotels nestled amongst the lush greenery. It is also possible to reach Ölü Deniz through Kayaköy, known in ancient times as Carmylessus. Kayaköy has remained deserted since 1925, when the Greeks living here immigrated back to Greece as a result of the population exchange that took place between the two countries. Buildings such as homes and a church in Kayaköy, which was once a relatively large town, are all in dilapidated condition.

As for getting from Fethiye to Ölü Deniz by sea, a course that would take you past both Şahin Burun and Dökükbaşı Burnu to the Karacaören Islands and from there, to Gemili Island. Gemili Island is an ideal location to drop anchor. This island as well as the Karacaören Islands are full of Roman and Byzantine ruins. There are ruins of a palace with mosaics at the top of the hill on Gemili Island, whereas there is also a 500-meter long tunnel that runs from the palace to the shore. In addition, one can make out the ruins of a

church and a house amongst the island flora. An earthquake struck the island in 240 A.D., knocking a portion of it into the sea. The island is also known as the Island of St. Nicholas from a church with the same name which is situated on it.

Ölü Deniz, which reminds one of paradise with its motionless sea surrounded by evergreen pines, is a tourism center known throughout the world. Besides the sea and the extraordinary hotels, one can also do some parachute gliding off the top of Mt. Babadağ, which towers above Ölü Deniz at a height of 1,975 meters. Next to Ölü Deniz is the wide sandy beach of Belceğiz. Three kilometers beyond Belceğiz is Kıdrak Cove with its sparkling sea which is surrounded by pine forests. Stretching back from this cove about 3-4 kilometers is Butterfly Valley, which is an interesting canyon with steep cliffs up to 350 meters high. It is called Butterfly Valley because of the fact that a particular species of butterfly called 'Jersey Tiger' is seen here every summer from July to September. The

An aerial view of Kayaköy.

other cities of antiquity that are near here can be visited as long as one is spending the night in Ölü Deniz.

The reason this heavenly place is called Ölü Deniz ("The Dead Sea") is attributed to the following legend; Once upon a time, a father and his son were caught in a storm here and were in danger of sinking. The son claimed that if they approached the rocks on the shore, they could take shelter in a cove. In the meanwhile, the father asserted that their ship would be driven onto the rocks and break up and that there were no coves around here anyway. Fearful of running aground onto the rocks, the father knocked his son, who was at the helm at the time, into the sea with an oar and took over the helm himself. Just as the ship was about to smash up on the rocky point, a calm bay opened up in front of him. This is why they say the bay is called Ölü Deniz. This bay, has a point at the back part of it, whereas vessels are not permitted inside the bay, which keeps water pollution to a minimum.

35

Saklı Kent

One reaches Saklı Kent by exiting the Fethiye-Antalya Highway after Kemer, where the signpost indicates the road to Saklı Kent. Driving down this road for 21 kilometers without turning off towards Tlos will lead you to Saklı Kent, which is located in a canyon on the slopes of Mt. Akdağ, 50 kilometers outside Fethiye.

One arrives in the canyon by passing over a wooden foot bridge that has been fastened to the cliff with 100-meter long steel rods. Crossing the icy-cold raging rapids on foot using a rope for guidance is as fun as it is scary. A total of 16 caves have been discovered in the rocks, which rise to a height of up to 600 meters, whereas prehistoric man encountered this place and used it for shelter.

Mr. Ekrem Uçar, who discovered Saklı Kent while herding sheep years ago in the nearby village of Kayadibi, now provides services to arriving visitors through organizing the surroundings. In addition, he also conveniently puts up those who arrive too late in the afternoon at his hotel that he had built through his own initiative and financing. Getting out of Fethiye's sweltering 40° C heat and into this very cool 18-kilometer long canyon and lunch on freshwater trout is bound to be one of the pleasures of a lifetime.

Eight kilometers into the canyon brings you to a small hill that the local villagers call Delikin. It is here, up above the canyon where one encounters the village of Arsaköy, which was established over the ancient city of Arsada. This means that the ancient

A view of Saklı Kent.

A sarcophagus in the village of Arsa, above Saklı Kent.

A different view of Saklı Kent.

name of Arsada has survived to our day as Arsa. Of the town itself none of the buildings remain, but in and around the village are a number of Lycian tombs, mostly of 'Gothic' sarcophagus type, one of which has human heads represented on each of its short sides; but most of them are now overthrown. There is at least one rock-tomb of house-type, and many sculptured and inscribed blocks are lying around. The inscriptions are almost all epitaphs.

A little above the village, beside the path from the north, on an outcrop of rock about two and a half meters high, is a relief representing a horse and rider. The horse is prancing to the right, his right hand is raised behind him and carries an elongated object of uncertain character, and he seems to have had a sword slung over his left shoulder. This looks like one of the Anatolian horseman-deities; the best known of these is Kakasbos, who appears frequently in western and northern Lycia; but he is excluded here, since he never carries a sword but always a club and his horse always proceeds at a gentle walk.

Cadyanda

18 kilometers north-east of Fethiye, at Üzümlü, is the site of Cadyanda. From Üzümlü, there is a long and steep climb in order to reach this city, from one and a half to three hours on foot. You will not regret that you had made the climb once you reach the top as you will be greeted with a commanding view as well as ruins of a theater, stadium, baths, temple and agora.

Cadyanda, 'Kadawanti' in Lycian, was never more than an obscure city. It is mentioned only once in ancient manuscripts, whereas its monuments and inscription go back to the 5th century B.C.

Perched on its hilltop 400 meters above Üzümlü and about 900 meters above the sea, Cadyanda was certainly in a commanding situation. The ancients Greeks, like the modern Turks, made light of a 300-meter climb at the end of their day's work. The more comfortable ascent leads round the hill from the north side by the east to the south; the more direct path is a very steep but convenient for the descent.

On the way up is a group of four handsome tombs; three of these, of house-type, are cut in large boulders which have fallen at a later stage and are now lying at odd angles. The fourth stands free on all four sides and appears to be cut from the solid rock;

The stadium of the ancient city of Cadyanda.

the two long sides are decorated with very fine reliefs-
-on the south side a man reclining on a couch, on the
north a mounted warrior riding over a fallen foe and
charging down another who carries a shield and a
spear raised ineffectually skyward. Sir Charles
Fellows dated this tomb to around 400 B.C. and called
it Hector's Tomb. The artist, George Scharf was
brought with him, whereas Scharf had painted a
picture of this tomb.

Approaching the site from the south, the
visitor comes first upon an immense number of tombs
or graves, most of which have been illicitly dug in
recent times and are consequently destroyed or badly
damaged; a few still stand more or less intact. Some
consist of a vaulted chamber originally covered with
plaster, a type common of Olympus on the east coast,
but not characteristic of Lycia as a whole.

A little further up is the city-wall, constructed
of wide stone blocks, fairly well preserved in this part,
but hardly discernible elsewhere. It still possesses an
impressive panoramic view of the Xanthos Valley and
the Fethiye Plain.

Just inside it is a small theater in poor
condition. Many of its seats survive on the west side,
and the semi-circular retaining wall of the cavea
stands all round; it is built against the excavated
hillside and is visible only from the interior. The
stage-building is a more or less unintelligible ruin.

Across the city center, from west to east, runs
a long open space some 10 meters wide and over 90
meters long, not unlike the main avenue in Phaselis.
Nevertheless, despite its dimensions and its unusual

*The Cadyanda
Amphitheater.*

39

Plan of Cadyanda

1. *Doric Temple*
2. *Baths*
3. *Stadium*
4. *Agora*
5. *Gymnasium*
6. *Amphitheater*
7. *City walls*

The Hector Sarcophagus in the vicinity of Cadyanda.

position, there is no doubt that this is a stadium. The city must have possessed a stadium, as the inscriptions mention two athletic festivals celebrated at Cadyanda. Eight statue-bases of athletic victors have been found in or around it, and six rows of seats are partially preserved on the north side; along the south side runs a line of blocks. Except at the west end it is much overgrown. The original length is in fact uncertain, as the ends are destroyed, and may have approximated more nearly to the standard length of some 200 meters.

Adjoining the stadium on the south is a building in ashlar masonry of the Roman period,

divided into three chambers, with three large windows on the south side. The western chamber has an apse at its south end. An inscription lying close by records that the Emperor Vespasian built the baths out of the money recovered by him for the city. We know nothing of course of the circumstances, but it is interesting to have this evidence of the interest taken by the emperor in the affairs even of the minor cities of his empire. The building in question must evidently be the baths though its form is unusual for a bath of the Roman period. The three chambers are now in a state of ruin, but a small building close to one corner is still standing in fairly good condition.

Across the way on the north side are the ruins of a large structure identified as a Doric temple, with stairs leading up to it from the stadium. However, there is little that can be made out of its present condition.

In the southwest part of the city, lost among

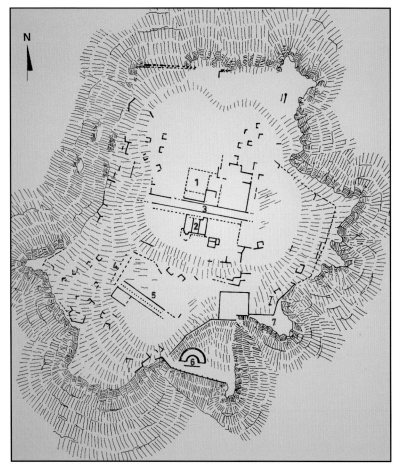

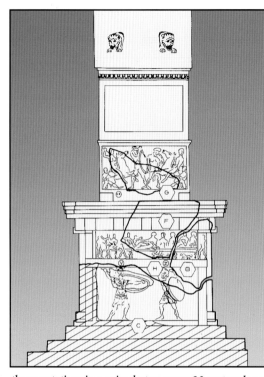

These included warriors, men and woman seated or reclining, and animals. On one side the male figures, but not the female, were identified by their name in Lycian or Greek; only one woman has a name attached, and she is called merely the 'wife of Zzala'. The tomb, which was quite possibly that of a Cadyandian princess who came from a Carian Hekatomnid family, is dated to the late 5th century B.C.

George Scharf drew a sketch of this monument showing the condition it was in at the time. In 1966, some of the pieces of this monument which were shipped off to the British Museum were examined in detail by Borchardt. Subsequent drawings were made.

A diagram of the Salas Monument (4th century B.C.). Some parts of the monument are found in the British Museum.

Ruins of Cadyanda.

the vegetation, is a ruined stoa some 90 meters long; the space adjoining it on the north has been dubiously identified as the agora. The city lays too high from an aqueduct of the normal Roman type, and a supply of water was secured by cisterns; many of these are to be seen, and half a dozen of them still contain water during the summer. On the whole, the site is very attractive but covered in overgrowth, and to some extent spoilt by illegal digging. At the foot of the hill, not far from Üzümlü, are two noteworthy tombs, one is called Hector and the other is Salas, though they are now sadly damaged. One stands near the road from Üzümlü to ancient city is a pillar-tomb of standard type but lacking the grave-chamber at the top.

It has recently been overturned and the upper stone is cracked in two. The other stood about a kilometer to the southeast of Üzümlü and was, among the most remarkable tombs in Lycia; it is now damaged almost beyond recognition. It was free-standing, cut from the rock, and carried reliefs on all four sides.

Tlos

To reach the ruins of Tlos, one exits the Fethiye-Kaş highway at the small town of Kemer and turn off the village of Kaleasar, where the ruins are situated.

We know that Lycia existed in the second millennium as the Lycian contribution to the Trojan wars is recorded (1200 B.C.). Generally speaking, however, records of Lycian cities go back as far as the 5th century B.C., whereas we cannot state with certainty when they were founded, saying only that Lycia existed much earlier than that, during the 2nd millennium, which seems to support this general evidence. Tlos was known to exist in the 2nd millennium, when it was called 'Talava,' whereas an axe was found by coincidence at the Tlos site that dates back to this period. Similarly, finds of this sort in other settlements in Lycia will allow us to preclude a date for the first settlements in each city. During the 2nd century B.C., we know that Tlos was a member of the Lycian League.

Two wealthy philanthropists were responsible for much of the city's building activity in the 2nd century A.D. One of these was Opramoas of Rhodiapolis, while the other was Licinnius Langurd of Oenoanda. The latter even aided Tlos with a sum of 50,000 denars.

Tlos was still inhabited during the Byzantine period, and is one of the few ancient towns which was able to maintain considerable status in the area until the 19th century.

The walls around the acropolis and the large ruined buildings date from the Ottoman period. The highest parts of the acropolis were inhabited by Kanlı Ali Ağa, and used by him as a winter quarters during the 19th century.

The wall to the east of the acropolis belongs to the Lycian period. To the east and north of the acropolis are the rock tombs, which form an impressive view from some distance. The necropolis of Tlos is contained within the Roman

Views of the rock tombs on the Tlos acropolis as well as those situated above.

A view of the
magnificent baths of
Tlos.

Plan of Tlos

1. Acropolis fortress
2-4. House-type
Lycian Tombs
5-6. Lycian Tombs
7. Lycian wall
8. Roman wall
9. Stadium
10. Gymnasium
11. Palaestra
12-13. Baths
14. Temple
15. Agora
16. Theater
17. Tower
18. Roman Necropolis
19-20. Roman
Sarcophagi
21. Byzantine Basilica
22. Byzantine Building.

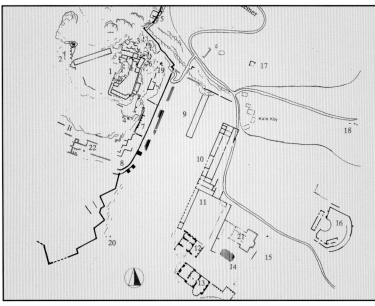

walls, whereas Lycian sarcophagi bearing inscriptions can be found here.

The Roman walls encircle the acropolis where it is left exposed without a natural rock wall. The eastern part of the outer stone walls is in sufficiently good shape to indicate their original monumental proportions. A gate pierces the walls at the south-eastern corner.

Almost all the main buildings of the city are situated outside the walls, including the stadium. This building, which was supported by the walls, contained 14 rows of seats. The building standing opposite the stadium, which has an entrance portal 4 meters' high, divided into three sections, and crowned with an arch, must have been a basilica. We notice that the last part of the wall to the east of

44

A house-type Lycian tomb situated above the Tlos Castle.

Situated above Tlos is Yaka Park.

this building had been used as an aqueduct.

At the southernmost part of the ruins are found the remains of the paleastra and the gymnasium, near the baths. In many Roman sites, these three buildings are found side by side. Next to the baths in this group is another bath which sports a circular terrace. This is a particularly magnificent building.

East of the gymnasium is a large Byzantine church. The heaps of rubble between the church and the baths most probably indicate the existence of a temple at that spot. The large terrace to the east was the site of the agora of Tlos.

A path leading eastwards from the village coffee-house takes us to the theater. The skene of

The Tlos Amphitheater, constructed during the Roman Age.

Today, the Tlos Stadium is overgrown with grass.

this theater was highly ornamented, and the theater as a whole has survived well. It was built by Opramoas for the sum of 60,000 denars. These days, a part of the inscription of the theater under the northern analemme wall together with a fragment of the Izrara Monument, dating from the Lycian period can be seen today. The actual monument has been removed to the Fethiye Museum. On it are portrayed highly dramatic battle scenes in relief including the mounted Izrara engaged in battle with a mounted soldier, the mounted soldier fighting a Hoplite, the battle of the Hoplites and the siege of the fortress. The fortress portrayed in the reliefs may possibly have been the Tlos Castle.

A large Roman tower, which has survived intact to the present, can be seen to the north of the square where the village coffee - house stands.

One can also find several sarcophagi scattered among the fields north of the theater which date from various periods.

Pınara

The Pınara Acropolis, where thousands of pigeon-type tombs are found.

The Pınara Amphitheater, which remains in a remarkably preserved state.

The name Pınara has survived, assimilated to the Turkish word for 'minaret', in the village of Minare half an hour below the ruins. The village is easily accessible via a short road that branches off the main Fethiye-Kaş Highway. Climbing up from the village, the visitor's eye is first caught by a great round mass of rock which seems to have given Pınara its name. In fact, Pınara means 'round' in the Lycian language.

According to ancient accounts, Pınara was founded by colonists from Xanthos. While it is necessary to mention Pınara along with the historical region, it surrendered to Alexander by opening its gates to him. Pınara's history goes back much further than Alexander, all the way back to Troy. Homer tells of the Lycian archer Pandarus who fought in the Trojan army. Strabo and later Stephanos Byzantions both mention that Pınara was Lycia's most important city.

Pınara, which was one of the six main cities of the Lycian League that possessed three votes, was annexed to the crown of Pergamon after the death of Alexander the Great, and subsequently went on to become a Roman town. It became remarkably prosperous and a number of important monuments were built during this period. Although it was inhabited as late as the 9th century, much of the settlement was destroyed by two earthquakes, in 141 and 240 A.D. respectively. Rocks that were knocked loose in the 1957 earthquake slid down the side of the mountain.

The acropolis is set on the top of the rock, and approached via a steep flight of steps from the south, carved into the rock. It is understood by examining the fortified Byzantine structures to the

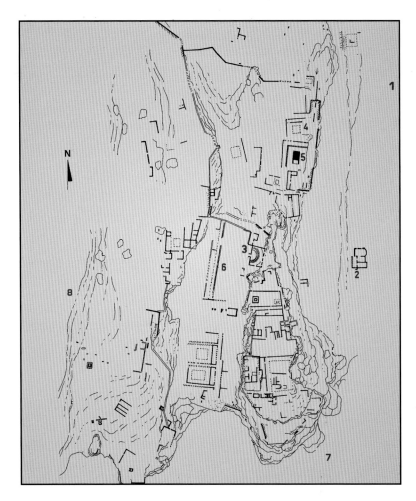

Plan of Pınara

1. Theater 2. Bath
3. Odeion 4. Temple
5. Tomb building
6. Agora 7. Necropolis
8. Rock tombs

Arttumpara Tomb in Pınara with an Amphitheater from the Roman Ages in the background. 4th century B.C.

This temple is thought to belong to Aphrodite, the Goddess of Love. In fact, the columns were heart-shaped, whereas a male penis was made into a relief.

West of this lies a structure thought to be a temple measuring 13 X 8 meters, on a podium, surrounded by a temenos, or a mausoleum, with a Lycian portal to the south, with typical pediment and lentil structure, opposite which stand the odeion of the settlement, entered through a portal to the east, and now in considerable ruin.

Heading towards the south and we come to a gate from the Lycian period with its door frame and lentil. The odeion, with its three entry portals from the east, is barely recognizable. The agora was reached via a gate from the orchestra of the odeion, and is set on a small plateau between two outcrops of rock, reinforced with terrace walls. The western face of the outcrop below the agora was carved out, presumably for the marking of tombs which were never completed. The remains of a palace, several Byzantine structures and cisterns are also found here.

Descending into the valley from the terrace walls in the southern flank of the agora, one encounters water channels cut into the rock, a spring, and the royal tombs all on the eastern side of the valley.

Pilinius, who had visited Pınara, qualified the Pınarians as being bird-men after seeing the tombs cut out of the stone. Among the reliefs to be found on rock tombs below the acropolis are those containing human figures on the facade, and representations of the Lycian cities before the crypt, which give us valuable information about the appearance of these ancient settlements. A similar

east of the settlement that it was in use until the end of the Byzantine period.

The ancient settlement of Pınara is situated in the eastern part of the acropolis. A number of fine structures indicating the prosperity of the town during ancient times were set on a series of terraces which are approached from the south-east by a flight of rock-cut steps, leading first to the remains of a Roman temple which contained six columns to the front and rear, and eight on the lateral facades.

A house-type Lycian tombs in Pınara.

relief was found among the reliefs of the Izrara monument at Tlos.

A nearby tomb bears reliefs containing a bovine, horned figure on the arched, saddle-like cover of the sarcophagus, which is similar to others in Kaş and Limyra. Situated to the east of the city lies a Greek-style theater, which has 27 seating rows divided by stairs into nine sections.

To the west and directly opposite the theater,

is a Lycian sarcophagus in good condition. It is understood from the three lines of inscription on this 4th century B.C. sarcophagus that it belonged to someone by the name of Arttumpara. One also notices the ruins of a bath between the theater and the other ruins.

In the extreme south of the site, in the hillside beyond the stream, are more rock-tombs, handsome and well deserving of a visit, though requiring something of an effort to reach.

Sidyma

The ruins of Sidyma are near the village of Dodurga, which is reached from the Fethiye-Kaş road by driving down the side road that turns off from Eşen for a distance of about 17 kilometers. If you continue from here, you will reach the ruined remains of Sidyma in the Asar district of the village.

The form of the name Sidyma (like Idyma, Didyma and Loryma) is proof enough of a high antiquity for the city. There is in fact some evidence on the site itself for occupation at least in the early classical period; but the first literary reference is not before the 1st century B.C., and the bulk of the ruins, and all the inscriptions are of the Roman Imperial Age. There exists, however, a silver coin of Lycian League type, apparently of Sidyma, which dates probably to the 2nd century B.C. The city continues to be listed by the geographers down to Byzantine times, but only a single historical account is recorded here.

Emperor Marcian (450-457 A.D.), at the time a simple soldier on a campaign against the Persians, fell sick on the way through Lycia and was left behind in Sidyma. There he was befriended by two brothers who took him into their home and nursed him; and one day, when he was recovered, they took him hunting with them. At midday, hot and tired, they lay down to sleep. One of the brothers, waking before his companions, was astonished to see that Marcian was sleeping in the sun and that an enormous eagle had settled on him and was shading him with its outstretched wings. When all were awake, the brothers asked Marcian, "If you become emperor, what favor will you grant us!" Marcian replied, "In that unlikely event I will make you Fathers of your city'. When he did in fact succeed to the purple on the death of Theodosius II, he remembered his promise and, going one better, appointed the brothers to high office in Lycia.

The acropolis hill, in two parts, lies on the north; along its south-east foot runs a stretch of early wall some 365 meters long and up to 3 meters high in places. The masonry is mostly regular ashlar, but polygonal at the east end, and at one point is a small gate with a forecourt and flanking tower. This wall provides the second piece of material evidence for an early city of Sidyma, set on the hill above.

Remarkably enough, no trace of this early city has survived on the hill; there are some walls, cisterns, and shards, but they are all of the Byzantine Age. There is, however, a little above the early wall a

One of the Lycian monument tombs found in Sidyma.

small theater or theater-like building, very badly preserved with six rows of seats partially visible at the back, but anything else which may have survived was buried under the earth and stones that have slipped down the hillside.

The city center, which is also the village center, lies at the west end of the site. There were once the remains of a temple and stoa here which were sufficient to permit a reconstruction on paper. The back wall of the stoa is still recognizable, but not much of the temple can now be made out. It was quite small, about 9 meters in length, with steps and four columns on the west front, and was dedicated to the Savior Gods the Emperors'. Part of the inscription of the stoa was also found, with a dedication to Emperor Claudius (41-54 A.D.), Artemis, and other deities.

A modern-day village Koran school is situated on the site of an ancient bath, the aqueduct leading to this building can be seen in the vicinity. Also seen in the village are the ruins of a church. A Lycian tomb can be seen in the garden of a village house to the

north of the village, surmounted by typical triglyphs and metopes. Not far from this is the Roman necropolis of the ancient settlement, containing a number of tombstones ornamented with reliefs and inscriptions.

Nearby is a row of sarcophagi, two of which especially catch the eye. They are identical in form and size and rest on a common base. Like the others in Sidyma they have a gable-shaped roof, with acroteria at the lower corners. The badly weathered inscriptions show that, as would be expected, the two tombs belong to members of the same family, apparently father and son, both bearing the name Aristodemus, which seems to have regularly repeated in the family.

A short distance to the south-west is a conspicuous building that still stands nine meters high. It rests on a low substructure which originally formed the base of a large built tomb, but the building itself is of much later date and contains many re-used blocks, some inscribed. There are a number of tombs of various types scattered along the valley in groups.

Lycian and Roman tombs lie side by side in Sidyma. A sarcophagus from the Roman Age is seen here (2nd century A.D.).

55

Xanthos

"The Persian army entered the plain of Xanthos under the command of Harpagos and did battle with the Xanthians. The Xanthians fought with small numbers against the superior Persian forces with legendary bravery. They resisted the endless Persian forces with great courage but were finally succumbed and forced to retreat within the walls of their city. They gathered their womenfolk, children, slaves and treasure into the fortress. This was then set on fire from below and around the walls, until all was destroyed by the conflagration. The warriors of Xanthos made their final attack on the Persians, their voices raised in their battle cries, until every last man from Xanthos was killed."

Only the Xanthians who happened to be in other places at the time were spared and it was they who returned at a later date to resurrect the city.

After reading this passage from Herodotus of Halicarnassus, we learn that Xanthos existed during the 6th century B.C. They fight as allies of the Trojans, coming *"from distant Lycia and the eddying Xanthos"*; their commander Sarpedon was among the minor heroes during the battles that took place in the 12th century B.C. This indicates to us that there was a Xanthos around 1200 B.C., as well. However, this hapless though magnificent city was completely burnt down between 475 and 450 B.C. During excavations, this was confirmed by a thick layer of ash covering the site. In 429 B.C., all of Lycia united against their Athenian satrap Melasandros, who wanted to impose new taxes on them. Melasandros died in this war and relations with Athens fizzled out. Xanthos was captured by Alexander the Great in 334 B.C. The Xanthians' dealings with him are a matter of uncertainty. The historian Appian, writing in the 2nd century A.D., records that 'they are said to have been unwilling to submit to him, and to have suffered as one the previous occasion, destroying themselves in the name of freedom.' This is not, however, confirmed by any other evidence, and Arrian, our most respectable authority for Alexander's campaign, also writing in the 2nd century, observes merely that Xanthos was surrendered to Alexander along with Pınara, Patara, and other places. Appian's hearsay account therefore should no doubt be rejected.

While Alexander was in the region, a prophecy is said to have occurred. A fountain near Xanthos suddenly welled up of its own accord and threw out a bronze tablet inscribed with archaic letters announcing the overthrow of the Persian Empire by the Greeks.

This is the first house-type Lycian tomb that one encounters in Xanthos.

A panoramic view of Xanthos from the Roman Acropolis.

The Xanthos Amphitheater which dates back to the Roman Age.

A mosaic decorating the floor of the Byzantine Church.

Alexander was encouraged by this to clear the whole coast of Persians as far as Cilicia.

In the confused period following Alexander's death, Xanthos came into the hands of Antigonus. Lycia was, however, claimed by the Egyptian king, and Ptolemy I came in 309 B.C. with a fleet and took it from him by force. Subsequently, we hear of the fortunes of Xanthos, which comes from an inscription, later erased but still just legible, on a jamb of the city's southern gate. This informs us that 'King Antiochus the Great dedicated the city to Leto, Apollo, and Artemis.' From this unusual text it is inferred that Antiochus III engaged in 197 B.C. in taking Lycia from the Ptolemies, finding himself unable to occupy

Another view of the Amphitheater.

A close-up of one of the mosaics found in the Byzantine Church.

Xanthos by force, made an agreement with the citizens, who were no doubt tired of being besieged, that they should make a nominal surrender of the city to him, on condition that he should consecrate it to the national deities of Lycia, that is in effect that he should declare it free and inviolable.

This benefit, however, was not of long duration. After Antiochus' defeat at Magnesia, Xanthos along with the rest of Lycia was given to Rhodes. An attempted tyranny at Xanthos in the 2nd century, which may have had Rhodian support, is mentioned above.

During the Roman civil wars of the 1st century B.C., the Xanthians staged their second (if it was not

their third) melodramatic holocaust. In 42 B.C., Brutus, who was engaged in raising forces and money for the forthcoming showdown with Octavian and Antony, came to Lycia. The Lycian League resisted him, but was defeated, and Brutus proceeded to besiege Xanthos. He demolished the Lycian acropolis and slaughtered its inhabitants. Plutarch recorded that after the fall of the city, a woman was seen hanging from a noose with her dead child slung from her neck, setting fire to the house with a burning torch. Hearing this, Brutus was moved to tears and proclaimed a reward for any of his soldiers who saved a Lycian from death. A bare 150 Xanthians fell alive into Roman hands.

The following year, Marc Antony, hoping to heal the scars left by Brutus, extended the hand of peace to the Xanthians by having their city rebuilt. Emperor Vespasian seemed to have treated the city with care, for a monumental arch in his name was erected in Xanthos. In Byzantine times the city-walls were renovated and a monastery built on top of the hill. The city had its bishop, though he ranked rather low under the metropolitan of Myra. It was deserted once the Arab raids started.

Xanthos was discovered in 1838 by Sir Charles Fellows, who had all the reliefs and archaeological finds of any significance transported to London on a warship that anchored in Patara. Many works of art from this site are now on display in the Lycian rooms of the British Museum. Excavations which have been ongoing since 1950 were undertaken by the French, then by Dr. Pierre Demarque, later taken over by Prof. Henri Metzger. The diggings are currently under the direction of Prof. Le Roy.

Xanthos is on the border of the Muğla and Antalya provinces, a natural boundary created by the Eşen Stream. It is situated near the village of Kınık, 55 kilometers from Fethiye. On the left as one ascends,

4th century B.C. tower monument with an 11-meter long inscription.

the slope near the village is the gateway to the city that was built during the Hellenistic Period. A little further on are the ruins of the Vespasian Arch.

On the right are the remains of the base of the Nereids Monument, which was carted off in sections and shipped to London. This Ionic-order structure, which dates back to 400 B.C., was in the form of a temple. Placed on a high pedestal measuring 10.15 meters x 68 meters x 5.15 meters high, it has two series of reliefs depicting battle scenes. Above the reliefs ran architectural ornamentation and an architrave supported on four columns. Friezes with scenes from everyday life decorate this architrave.

Between the columns were situated statues of sea fairies or 'Nereids' for which the temple was named. The Hellenistic walls encircle the city of Xanthos and are reinforced by towers added at various periods, whereas the eastern flank of the battlements dates from the 4th century B.C.

In place of the present theater stood the Lycian acropolis, whereas the acropolis is surrounded by a wall dating back to the 5th century B.C., with polygonal stones worked into it. Directly across from this is the Roman acropolis. Let's wander around the Lycian acropolis, the site where the Roman theater stands, which we encounter as soon as we enter. As it stands this was built in the mid-second century A.D.; a handsome donation of 30,000 denars by Opramoas of Rhodiapolis was earmarked specifically 'for the construction of the theater'. Located nearby are three splendid monuments, one of which is a Lycian pillar-tomb. Standing 4.35 meters high, this monument was built during the 4th century B.C., but was carried to its present site during the erection of the theater in the Roman period. Water from the village of Çay, which is located 15 kilometers from Xanthos, was brought here via an aqueduct, the cistern of which is found on the Lycian acropolis.

The famous Harpies Monument in Xanthos. Reliefs from the monument are on display at the British Museum whereas plaster-of-Paris copies are found in their place (c.480 B.C.).

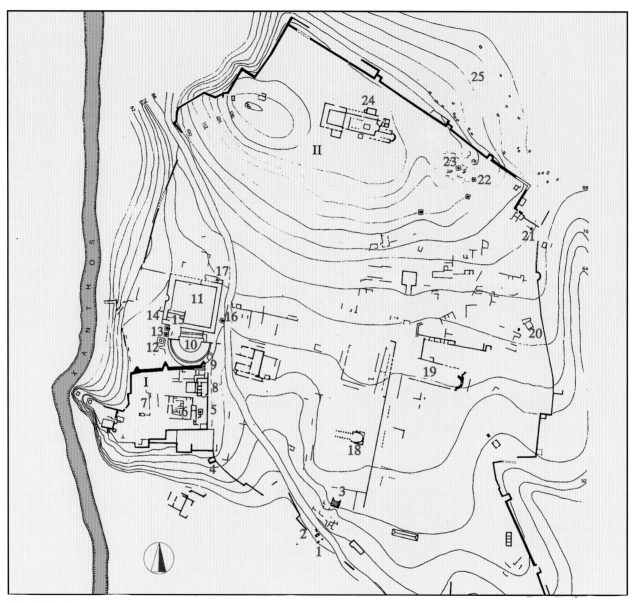

Plan of Xanthos

1. City Gate, Hellenistic 2. Vespasian Gate 3. Nereids Monument 4. Hellenistic Wall 5. Polygonal Wall 6. Lycian Palace 7. Lycian Buildings 8. Byzantine Church 9. Lycian Tomb, Columned 10. Roman Theater 11. Roman Agora 12. Roman columned Tomb 13. Lycian Tomb 14. Monument of the Harpies 15. Byzantine Basilica 16. Lycian Monument 17. Column with Inscription 18. Church 19. Basilica with Mosaics 20. Tomb of the Dancers 21. Lion Tomb 22. Payava Monument 23. Lycian Tomb 24. Byzantine Monastery 25. Merehi Sarcophagus.

An overall view of the Byzantine Church which contains mosaics.

On the western flank of the theater, which is remarkably preserved and carries the characteristics of the Roman Age, are three rather flashy monuments. The first one of these dates from the 1st century A.D. and is a Roman pillar-tomb; the second monument is a Lycian pillar-tomb, which sits on a high base, has a total height of 8.59 meters and was constructed in the 4th century B.C. The third monument is that of the famous Harpies Tomb, thusly called since Fellow's time through a dubious interpretation of its reliefs. The whole monument, measuring 8.87 meters high, has a base 5.43 meters in height. Large square lifting-bosses have been left projecting on three sides. The chamber at the top was of marble and decorated with reliefs; they were removed by Fellows and the covering stones propped up with wooden struts and a pile of stones. The tomb remained in this mutilated condition until 1957, when Turkish authorities installed the cement casts which have done much to restore the beauty of the monument. The reliefs are interesting, but, as often, not easy to understand. On all four sides are seated figures receiving gifts, on the south and east sides a bird, on the north a helmet; on the west side are two seated females, that on the right approached by three standing figures, the other receiving an indistinct object. On the east side are three other female figures, that on the right apparently accompanied by a dog. The figures which have given the tomb its name are on the north and south sides on either side of the seated figures; they represent bird-women with female heads, wings and tails, carrying children in their arms. When the tomb was first discovered, these were recognized as Harpies carrying off the daughters of Pandareos, as described by Homer: the children were left orphaned and were befriended by Hera, Athena, Artemis, and Aphrodite; when Aphrodite went to Olympos to arrange a suitable marriage for them, leaving them unprotected, the Harpies came and snatched them away to be servants of the Furies. That Pandarus was a Lycian hero seemed to give support to this interpretation. But there are difficulties. Pandarus and Pandareos are two different heroes; the latter had two daughters, not four; and the children on the relief are obviously not of marriageable age. More recently scholars have preferred to see in the winged females the other bird-women of mythology, the Sirens, carrying the souls of the dead, in the form of children, to the Isles of the Blessed. The seated figures are then members of the dynastic family; formerly Hera and Aphrodite were recognized on the west side, and Artemis with her hound on the east. All the reliefs were originally colored, chiefly in red and blue, traces of which were visible at the time of the discovery. On the back of the

relief-slabs were painted crosses and other symbols, suggesting that at some time the grave-chamber was used as a refuge by some Christian anchorite.

To the rear of these monuments is an agora dating from the Roman Period. On the corner facing the tombs is a Byzantine basilica. Behind the 2nd century A.D. agora at a northeast angle is the famous Xanthian Obelisk. 'Obelisk' is not in fact a good name for it, as it is simply a pillar-tomb of perfectly normal type. The upper type has suffered a good deal of damage, but many of the fragments have been recovered by the excavators; they show that the tomb possessed the usual grave-chamber, enclosed like the Harpy Tomb by slabs with reliefs showing the dead man, surely one of the dynasts, victorious over his enemies. The topmost block of the roof bears marks of the feet of a statue, no doubt the dynast himself. But the fame of the monument derives from the inscription which covers all four faces of the stone; it is the longest Lycian inscription known, running to over 250 lines. Linguistically it falls into three parts; beginning on the south side it continues on the east and part of the north side in the normal Lycian language; then follows a poem of twelve lines in Greek; but the rest of the north side and whole of the west is couched in that strange form of Lycian which appears elsewhere only on a tomb in Antiphellos.

As was said above, the Lycian language is little understood apart from the frequently repeated epitaph formulae; the present inscription, on the other hand, evidently gives a narrative account of the dead hero's exploits, and is still undeciphered. It does, however, contain a number of recognizable proper names, from which the approximate date and some idea of the contents may be gathered. The hero in question is called, in the Lycian and in the Greek, son of Harpagus (not of course the Persian general of the 6th century); his own name is lost in both places, but

The Monument of the Harpies (c. 480 B.C.) and the Lycian Tower Tomb (4th century B.C.)

he appears to be the Xanthian dynast, known from the coins, who appears several times elsewhere in the inscription in the Lycian form *Kerei*. In the Greek epigram, he is said to have been a champion wrestler in his youth, to have sacked many cities, slain seven Arcadian Hoplites in a day, set up more trophies than any other man, and added glory to the family of

Karikas. This Karikas appears as *Keriga* seven times in the Lycian; he too is known from the coins as a Xanthian dynast. Both he and *Kerei* are dated to the latter part of the fifth century B.C. And to this same period belong the historical name recognizable in the Lycian. In addition to Athenians and Spartans, Darius and Artaxerxes, we have more especially a mention of the Athenian Melasandros, who was sent to Lycia in 430-429 B.C. to collect tribute and prevent the Spartans from intercepting the Athenian corn ships. He failed and was killed in battle. It is likely that his defeat was among the exploits of *Kerei*.

In the southeast corner of the Lycian acropolis are the foundations of a square building comprising several rooms which is thought to have been the palace of the dynasts in the earliest times, destroyed at the time of the capture by Harpagus. It was replaced by another building of which the basement survives; the upper parts were apparently of wood. This was destroyed by fire in 470 B.C. and was not replaced. Higher up to the west is a small sanctuary with three parallel chambers, and the scanty remains of a temple of the Lycian equivalent of the Greek Artemis. At the west extremity stood a building which must originally have been very handsome; its architecture seems to have imitated the wooden houses whose features appear also in the tombs of house-type, and was decorated with a sculptured frieze; the blocks of this frieze were re-used by the Byzantines for repair of the acropolis wall, and were later removed to London by Fellows. Just to the northwest of this building is a rectangular foundation on which stood a pillar with a pediment on two sides; this too has gone into the Byzantine wall.

Most of the northeastern part of the acropolis is occupied by an extensive monastery. This includes a church set against the east acropolis wall, and to the west of this an open courtyard with wash-basins along one side. There are several mosaics in the Lycian acropolis. One of these mosaics has the famous scenes of the Calydon hunt as well as Thetis drowning

Achilles in the river Styx. Today, they are on display at the Antalya Museum. However, remains of the mosaic can be seen on the floor. For example, one can see the Leda and swan scene on the exterior of the southeast corner of the city walls.

Directly across from the Lycian acropolis is the Roman acropolis. Let's examine the artifacts here by walking in an eastern direction. We first encounter a Byzantine basilica. This incredible structure of which Lycian Age stones were used, is a basilica with three aisles. Some of the steps where the choir would stand in the apse can still be seen. In the apse's northern section is a polygonal-shaped room with marble plates of geometric motifs on the floor, whereas one encounters a fountain in the middle of the room. The entire floor of the basilica is covered entirely in mosaics, whereas there is a cistern under the middle aisle.

After seeing the wall remains of the agora across from the basilica, and walk towards the east one shall see the Belly-Dancer's Sarcophagus. War is depicted on one of the lid's long faces, while a hunting scene is seen on the other. As for the lid's two narrow faces, they depict two belly dancers turning towards each other. For this reason, this mid-4th century B.C. sarcophagus has been called the "Belly-Dancer Sarcophagus". From here, if we walk along the length of the north wall, we shall encounter of the pedestal of the Lion Pillar amongst the bushes at the corner where the wall turns. The upper portion is in the British Museum. In coming into the clearing, one comes across the necropolis where numerous sarcophagus can be seen.

The house-type tombs amongst the rocks are rather interesting. The Lion's Tomb and the Merihi Monument are the most striking tombs here. The Lion's Tomb, which depicts reliefs show lions attacking a bull, dates back to 480-450 B.C. The sarcophagus lid, which is not in its place, depicts a wild boar hunt on one face and a feast scene on the other face. Just beyond

this is the overturned pedestal of the Merihi Sarcophagus, which dates to 390 B.C. The sarcophagus lid was transported to the British Museum in the year 1840 by Sir Charles Fellows. One sees chariots pulled by four horses in a struggle against the Chimaera monster on both sides of the lid, which has the word "Merihi" inscribed on it.

A drawing of the Payava Sarcophagus (370-360 B.C.), which was shipped off to the British Museum in 1842. Its name comes from the fact that the name 'Payava' is written on it. (Charles Fellows, 1839)

A tower tomb from the 4th century B.C. in the Roman Acropolis.

The Lion's Tomb (c. 480 B.C.).

Looking at the rock tombs next to the Merihi Sarcophagus, let's go inside the wall. There are four monument tombs next to each other. The most striking of the four is the Lycian pillar tomb which was built from dressed stone during the 4th century B.C. It has three steps leading to the burial chamber, the floor of which is faced with marble. The facade, constructed in the Ionic order, measures 6.39 meters high. A little further on is the site of the Payava tomb, which dates from 370-360 B.C. It was transported in its entire state to London by Sir Charles Fellows in 1842, whereas there remains a very small part of the pedestal in a rather dismal state. On one face of the monument one can find a Lycian inscription of two sentences which mentions the name of the Persian Satrap

The Byzantine Basilica above the Roman Acropolis.

The part of the pedestal which remains from the Merehi Sarcophagus (c. 390 B.C.).

Autophradates.The other face has a relief of a war scene and a one-sentence Lycian inscription on the top part which states that the tomb was a work of Payava. On the long carved sides of the sarcophagus lids are reliefs with four horses pulling a chariot.

South of the Payava Sarcophagus lies another 4th century sarcophagus which is plainer than the others. There is a magnificent Lycian sarcophagus, known as the Ahqqadi Sarcophagus, which stands to the west of these tombs.

After seeing these, we can pass by a Byzantine basilica at the top of the acropolis which was built over an ancient Roman temple. From here we can return to the parking lot.

Letoon

The ruins of Letoon are situated in the village of Bozoluk. They can be reached by driving along a four-kilometer stretch of road that exits off the Kaş-Fethiye Road before Kınık.

The city of Letoon was founded in honor of Leto, who was the mother of Apollo and Artemis. Zeus, the father of the gods, falls in love with Leto. Hera, Apollo's jealous wife, has her followed and prevents her from giving birth to the children whom Zeus has fathered. Finally, Leto gives birth to Apollo and Artemis on Delos, and escapes to Lycia, on the Anatolian coast, away from Hera. Later, Delos was indicated as the birthplace of Apollo, but perhaps, as Leto said, she really gave birth at Patara.

The cult of Apollo was based on that of an Anatolian god and was initiated in Patara. As the cult spread, many places were adopted as his birthplace, among them the most widely accepted being Delos. It has often been said that many of the Greek gods were exported to Greece from Anatolia and were developed from the religious culture of the Hittites. This idea was popularized by the Turkish poet, Azra Erhat, the Fisherman of Halicarnassus as well as the writer of this book. Similarly, Artemis was considered a continuation of the Cybele cult, under a new name, and the clearest evidence of this is the Artemis Temple at Ephesus. It is accepted that Leto, the mother of these gods, was Anatolian and that she merged with Cybele.

Letoon, founded by the mother of Artemis and Apollo, the twin children of Zeus, was the sacred cult center of Lycia. We can trace settlement at Letoon as far back as the 7th century B.C. Excavations were begun by Dr. H. Metzger in 1962, and later on, continued under the direction of M. Christian Le Roy.

As one can see, the excavation site covers an area containing three temples placed side by side. The first of these, of the Ionic order, was dedicated to Leto and constructed towards the end of the 5th century B.C. through the efforts of King Arbinas. This has six

Views of the Temples of Leto, Apollo and Artemis, found in Letoon.

columns on the front and rear facades and eleven on each side. To either side of this temple are two small temples dedicated to Apollo and Artemis.

An inscription which was uncovered near a flight of steps cut into the rock north of the temples refers to Artemis in the Lycian language as Ertemit, which suggests that the second temple, which dates to the 4th century B.C., belonged to Artemis.

The third temple, which was constructed in the Doric order, belonged to Apollo. A mosaic discovered flanking the main temple, which is in nearly unrecognizable form, shows the bow and quiver of Artemis and the lyre of Apollo. In addition, many inscriptions were found among the foundations of the temples at Letoon during excavation. Of these, one of the most important is a multi-lingual inscription containing texts in Aramaic, Greek and Lycian. This inscription, which dates to 358 B.C. and is currently in the Fethiye museum, is very important in that it helped experts to decipher the Lycian language. It refers to a decree made by Pixodares, who was the satrap of Caria and Lycia.

To the south and west of the main temple excavation has revealed a large nymphaeum connected with the sacred spring. A rectangular building facing east-west is bordered by a large semi-circular paved basin, 27 meters in diameter and flanked on the north by two semi-circular exedrae. It dates to the time of Emperor Hadrian (117-138 A.D.) and replaces an earlier Hellenistic building. The excavation was conducted largely underwater, and the greater part is now permanently flooded. Part of the nymphaeum was later overlaid by a church, apparently dating to the 6th century.

A view of the porticoes of Letoon, which is covered in water from time to time.

The Letoon Amphitheater, which dates to the Roman Age.

Decorative details of the Leto Temple.

Plan of Letoon

1. *Temple of Leto*
2. *Temple of Artemis*
3. *Temple of Apollo*
4. *Church*
5. *Nymphaeum*
6. *West Portico*
7. *Hellenistic and Roman Portico*

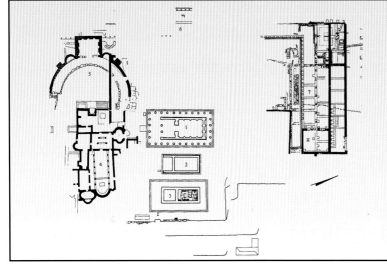

Letoon also had a stoa and a theater, whereas the existence of a stadium, although as yet untraced, is known, proving that this was not only a cult center, but also a living city.

The theater lies opposite the temples, resting on the slope behind, with an entrance visible to one side. This theater belongs to the Hellenistic Period. The arches to the east and west were decorated with Doric friezes and the auditorium was in good condition when excavation began although the skene building was completely destroyed.

Besides the fact that Letoon was a religious center, proof that it was also a place where people lived is shown with the finding of the theater, as well

76

A striking view of architectural remains found in Letoon.

Bow, arrow, sun and lyre mosaics uncovered at the Temple of Apollo.

as the stoa and stadium, which have yet to come to the light of day.

To the north of the precinct is a large and well-preserved theater of Hellenistic date. The cavea, which faces northwest, is more than a semicircle and in its middle part is cut out of the hillside; the ends are built of regular smooth-faced ashlar. There is one diazoma. A vaulted passage leads to the cavea on either side; that on the southwest end has on its inner face a row of 16 masks, representing among others Dionysus, Silenus, a satyr, a girl, and a funny old woman.

Letoon was a center of cult activity and an inhabited settlement until the 7th century, when it was subsequently abandoned.

Patara

The ancient city of Patara is situated between Fethiye and Kalkan, in the southwest corner of the plentiful Xanthos Valley. Exit off the main road onto the Gelemiş Road, then drive down this road for five kilometers until you reach the ruins of Patara. The finding of coins and ceramic fragments in recently carried out excavations that date back to the 7th century B.C., has given us reason to take Patara's history back even further.

Patara is renowned as the birthplace of

The Roman Sarcophagus next to the city gates.

The city gate (100 A.D.), which has become the symbol of Patara.

Apollo and is one of the oldest and most important cities of Lycia. The Hittite King Tudhalia IV (1250-1220 B.C.) was known to have said, *"I made sacrifices and presented gifts while facing Patar Mountain, I erected stelai, and constructed sacred buildings."* What we understand from this is that Patara was known during the Hittite Age as Patar.

As the principal port on the coast of Lycia, Patara has a long history. For this reason future excavations are bound to bring the city's ancient history to light. We know that the city existed in the 5th-6th centuries B.C. and that it was saved from destruction when it opened its gates to Alexander. During the wars of Alexander's successors, Patara enjoyed considerable importance as a naval base, in which capacity it was occupied by Antigonus in 315 B.C. and by Demetrios at the time of his siege of Rhodes in 304. In the 3rd century B.C., the city came with the rest of Lycia under Egyptian control. For a period it bore the Egyptian name Arsinoe; this name did not survive beyond the Egyptian rule. Patara was re-captured by Antiochus III in 190 B.C., Livius uttered the saying "Caput gentis", that is, "The Ancestors' Capital" to describe Patara, which exalted it above all the other cities.

Patara had a three-vote right in the Lycian League, like the cities of Xanthos, Tlos, Olympos and Myra. The League generally held its league conferences in Patara, which was its harbor as well. Patara, which didn't lose its importance during the Roman Empire, was also the seat of the Roman provincial governor, who turned it into a port from

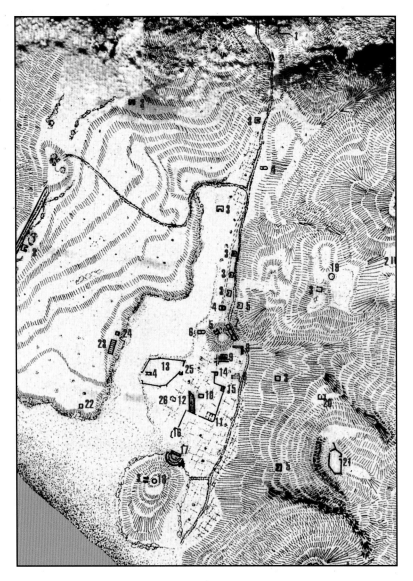

Plan of Patara *(Akdeniz University's Archaeology Department of Lycia Civilizations Research Center)*

1. Tower 2. Bridge 3. Monumental Tomb 4. Church 5. Rock-cut Tomb 6. Basilica
7. Tepecik Necropolis 8. Arch 9. Hurmalık Thermae 10. Central Baths
11. Vespasian Therme 12. Main Avenue 13. Byzantine City 14. Itinerarium
15. Marciana Tomb 16. Ecclestrion 17. Theater 18. Cistern 19. Oil Press
20. Water-pressure System 21. Acropolis 22. Lighthouse 23. Granarium
24. Temple Tomb 25. Corinthian Temple 26. Small Bath

which the Roman fleet maintained contact with the eastern provinces. In the meantime, Patara was the harbor where crops harvested in Anatolia were stored and kept for shipment to Rome. As in Andriace, silos were built here to store grain during the reign of Emperor Hadrian, who had visited Patara with his wife Sabina and stayed there for a short period.

During the Roman Age, Patara, which became the capital of both the Lycian and Pamphylian provinces, also became famous as one of Apollo's soothsaying centers.

Ancient writers refer to Patara as the birthplace of Apollo as well as the home of an important oracle, who they say interpreted omens during the winter in Patara and during the summer in Delos. During the Byzantine period, Patara again lost none of its importance, and became a Christian center of some significance, as St. Nicholas, whom we know as Santa Claus, was born here. St. Paul set out for Rome by boarding a ship from Patara. However unfortunately, subsequent to this period, apparently rejected by the gods and saints alike, the harbor of Patara, which was 1,600 meters long and 400 meters wide, silted up which prevented sea-going vessels from entering it. This meant that the city gradually lost its importance. Since then the city has gradually been covered with sand dunes, which has given it the appearance of a desert resulting in the slow obliteration of all the ruins left standing.

In recent years Prof. Fahri Işık and his team from Akdeniz University have been trying to dig this spellbinding city out from under the sand. Let's take a walk together through one of the most famous cities in history.

On the way to Patara, we may see the remains of Roman tombs by the side of the road,

Panoramic view of the Hurmalık Thermae.

Patara's Main Avenue, which is the widest avenue to have been uncovered in the excavations up to now.

about knee-high, and several tombs of the Lycian type, which indicate that this was the site of a necropolis. We also notice a monumental gate still standing which was the entrance to the city. According to its inscription, this victory arch was built in 100 A.D. by the Roman governor, Mettius Modestus. At the same time, this arch was used as a part of the aqueduct that brought water to Patara. Before arriving at the victory arch, one can see the monument tombs situated in the lower part of the road, along the edge of the lake, which has taken the place of the ancient harbor. These magnificent tombs have survived for the most part to this day. From here one may notice the harbor church, measuring 12 x 9.10 meters, with three aisles. This church remains submerged in water for most of the year.

There are many temples in Patara. A large bust of Apollo was discovered on the hill beyond the city gate, which indicates the existence of an Apollo Temple, the whereabouts of which are still not clear.

In fact, what we do know is that during the

first century of Roman rule, the center of the oracle of Apollo fell into disrepair, but that Opramoas, a rich Lycian whose name is to be seen throughout Lycia and who himself came from Rhodiapolis, had the town of Patara resurrected. Though the birthplace of the god Apollo, who was the child of Zeus and Leto, may be shown to be several places, it is accepted that he was born in Patara. Apollo is an Anatolian god.

In the Iliad, Homer mentions him as "Phoibos", which means 'illuminated', and 'the famous Lycian archer, Apollo.' For this reason, he along with his Anatolian sister, Artemis had always aided the Trojans and their Anatolian city, Troy. The name 'Lycia' meant 'illuminated nation' in ancient times, whereas their head god, Apollo, was perceived to have light in his lineage. Right next to the victory arch is a sarcophagus from the Roman period. To the west of the sarcophagus are the ruins of the Date Baths. With its floor decorated with thick stones and mosaics, these baths were called Date Baths due to the giant date trees next door. These baths belonged

The ancient harbor of Patara, which has become a marsh. The grain silo and other structures are seen opposite side of the marsh.

83

The Roman Amphitheater (c. 2nd century A.D.)

to the Roman period, and were also used during the Byzantine Age. One hundred meters ahead is a road sign measuring 2.35 m. long x 1.60 wide x 5.50 m high. This road sign, which was discovered in recent excavations, was made by Quintus Veranius on the orders of Emperor Claudius and it is extremely important as it shows the distances between the Lycian cities. This is the world's oldest and most comprehensive road sign.

Walking along the asphalt road, we come to some ruins of a church at the side of the road. It is understood that the church was constructed with previously used stones from the architectural fragments in the inner walls.

Walking just beyond this church, one encounters the tomb of Marciana in the middle of the wall, whereas one may find the Vespasian Baths in the western corner of this tomb. They are called the Vespasian Baths on account of the money he had put aside for their construction. The baths measure 105 x 48 meters and were partitioned into five sections. In order to see inside the baths you need to step over the large stones. If we stay on the footpath next to the baths, we shall reach Anatolia's widest main avenue, which was 12.5 meters in width and covered in marble. Under the main avenue was a high quality sewage network. There are stoa lined up along the western part of the main avenue, which

Two different views of the ancient city of Patara.

opens out to several roads, Today, this main avenue spends most of the time underwater. The city's central baths are located at the eastern end of the avenue, whereas there are ruins of a small baths complex at the western end.

A little further along the road and we encounter the wide walls of a Byzantine fortress. To the east of this fortress is a Corinthian temple that was constructed from well arranged stones, the owner of which is unknown. Measuring 13 x 11 x 6.10 meters this 2nd century A.D. 'in antis' plan temple, had plenty of architectural ornamentation.

The theater, which is set into a slope, is unfortunately half-buried in sand. A team from

Akdeniz University has been continuing its excavation studies and just like other sites around Patara, has been removing the sand from the theater. An inscription on the eastern side of the skene indicates that it was built by Velia Prouila and her father in 147 A.D.

North of the theater is what was known as Anatolia's largest administration building (the ecclesterium), which measures 43 m long by 29 m wide. At the top of the hill behind the theater is a monument tomb, whereas, nearby is an 8-meter deep cistern that has been carved into the rock. To the west of the cistern is a part of the walls of the harbor lighthouse of Patara.

Hadrian's Granary can be seen in a swamp next to the harbor. This building, called the horrea or granarium, measured 67 x 19 meters and was divided into eight sections.

Next to this, one can encounter a large temple-tomb that is still intact. This temple tomb, which was constructed from thick and showy stones, must have been quite magnificent during ancient times. From here, there are a number of monument tombs of various sizes stretching all the way out to the village. In addition, there are tombs to be found on the hill opposite the ticket office. The marshy reeds in the lake that used to be a harbor in ancient time whisper about the splendor of ancient Patara.

We believe that new discoveries will continue to occur in the new excavation work currently taking place in Patara, whereas one day, the sleeping Patara is going to achieve the fame she deserves.

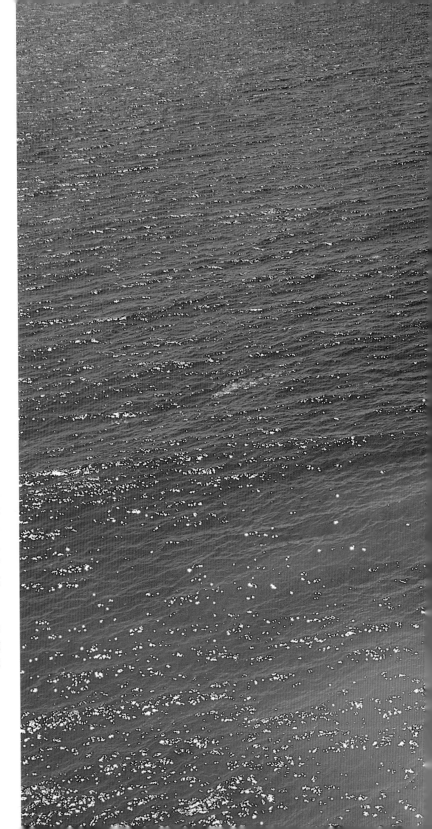

A view of Kapıtaş Beach, near Kalkan, which attracts people with its fine sand and crystal clear water.

Kalkan

Despite the fact that it holds no historical artifacts, Kalkan, which is connected to Kaş, it is a highly sought after tourism center. Known as *Kalamaki* in ancient times, Kalkan is on the Kaş-Fethiye Highway, 25 kilometers out of Kaş.

In the population exchange of 1925, the people living here migrated to either Greece or Australia. Those that left for Greece promptly set up a village near Athens they named 'Kalamaki' and continued in their ways. Their children occasionally come and visit Kalkan to catch up on things that have taken place in their old community. This provincial district, which up to recently had derived its income from making soap and olive oil, has, thanks to its spotless pensions and hotels and restaurants, which serve up some delicious dishes, became a favorite stopover place for blue voyagers. Yachts sailing past Yedi Burun, which sticks out into the sea like a sharp point, can slip into Kalkan's safe harbor. Just as the town is able to meet all your provision needs, you'll also have the opportunity to visit the sites of three important Lycian cities, Patara, Letoon and Xanthos all within one day.

Tourists staying in Kalkan can visit Kapıtaş Cave, which is located six kilometers from the town. Measuring 50 x 40 x 15, the cave is rather impressive by the way sunlight is reflected into the cave to produce incredible hues of green and blue. The cave is big enough to wander through it in a small motorboat, whereas there is the nearby Kapıtaş Beach as well, which is an ideal spot to take a dip in the sea.

Because it shelters so many pigeons, the cave behind Ince Burun and two kilometers from Kalkan is known as the Güvercinlik Sea Cave. Both the small, narrow mouthed Güvercinlik İni and the Deniz Cave are 100 meters from the Güvercinlik Cave. The road goes as far as Inbaş cave, on the Bezirgan Village shoreline near Kalkan. Kalkan is a good rest spot with its quaint whitewashed buildings that have been turned into pensions and restaurants over the past several years. They look fabulous in spring, decked out with purple and red bougainvillea flowers.

Two different views of Kalkan.

Two separate views of the bougainvillea-filled streets of Kalkan.

Daily excursions to nearby locations can be made from Kalkan. For instance, a good place for trekking is the Bezirgan Plateau, which is situated just above Kalkan. Ruins of an ancient city called Pirha can be seen in the hills above the village of Bezirgan, which is full of greenery.

Trekking 15 minutes from the village, one reaches the remains at a height of 850 meters above sea level. The mountain cliff is full of several stone-tombs. As for sarcophagi, they are seen scattered in a sloppy manner. At Göldağ, on the border of the two villages of Bezirgan and Islamlar, one finds incredibly worked stone tombs that are interconnected to each other. Exiting the village of Bezirgan on the way to Gömbe, one encounters a Lycian house-type tomb

A view of the Kalkan Marina.

A Lycian tomb with reliefs which is found on the Bezirgan Village Road near Kalkan.

that has been carved into the rock opposite a plane tree. This tomb, which was decorated with both inner and outer reliefs, is currently in a damaged state.

Continuing down this road, one arrives in the village of Sütleğen, which shelters a myriad hues of green. A little below this point are the Nisa ruins in a place called Meryemlik. One will not see much more than the rubble of the theater, the ancient road that passed through here as well as sarcophagi.

Passing through Sütleğen, this road takes us to Gömbe. Gömbe, which has an abundant supply of water, is famous for its Uçansu Waterfalls and Yeşilgöl. The ruins of ancient Chomba are located in Gömbe.

91

Phellos

In order to reach Phellos, which is located on the Felen Plateau, you need to exit the Kaş-Finike Highway at Ağullu, towards Çukurbağ to Pınarbaşı, which is reached either via the newly-opened 3-kilometer stretch of road or the other road a little further up ahead.

One of the many sarcophagi found in Phellos.

From here, one needs to go as far as the fire observation tower. We can leave our car here and start walking towards the hill which is located just ahead. In addition, it is possible to reach the ruins by trekking from Kaş. The acropolis on the hill can be reached via the narrow footpath which is hidden amongst the bushes. Looking down from the acropolis, we can see that we are directly above Kaş. Looking west, we are enchanted by the view of the snowy peak of Mt. Akdağ.

Phellos was a rather significant town in the 4th century B.C. In fact, Antiphellos, (today's Kaş) was Phellos harbor. Later, while Antiphellos was becoming a rich and important town on account of its cedar forests, Phellos lost its old importance.

The city occupies a long narrow area on the crest of the hill, some 550 meters in length and 150 meters in width. The first indication of it on the way up is a group of four sarcophagi in a row, with a fifth now fallen. A little above this, several stretches of the north wall of the city are standing, in massive polygonal masonry of early date; on the south side the wall is almost entirely destroyed down to ground-level, though its line is recognizable in places. The highest point is occupied by an enclosure with a rough wall surrounding a hollow now filled with scrub; this apparently represents a medieval fortification of the summit.

Below the city-wall on the south side is a very handsome sarcophagus still largely intact. It stands on a solid base and has reliefs on three sides. On the long south side is a man reclining on a couch holding a cup, with a figure standing on either side of him; in front of him is a table, and below the couch are two birds resembling pheasants. On the short west end is a man, apparently a warrior, but partly destroyed by a large hole broken into the tomb, and on the lid above two facing griffins in the two panels; on the other short end is a man standing with arms outstretched, while a smaller figure on the left hands him a helmet.

There are a number of rock-cut Lycian tombs on the south slope of the hill, some partly buried; at least one has a Greek inscription of the Roman period.

Towards the west end is a free-standing tomb of house-type cut entirely from the rock; it contains a single chamber with benches on three sides, the one at the back is hollowed out. Two fragments of a Lycian epitaph were found close by. Just to the east of this is a curious and interesting complex, comprising a house-tomb with two chambers, outer and inner, in good preservation, other small tombs of various kinds more or less broken, a semi-circular wall of late masonry, and a rock-wall carrying a relief of a huge bull, which has seen a great deal of damage .

Alone among the cities of the region, that on Mt. Felen is very well supplied with water. There is a copious spring on the east slope of the hill, and a fountain in the village of Çukurbağ; not far away, at Pınarbaşı, is a particularly abundant spring which today supplies Kaş. And on the hilltop, inside the city-walls, two wells have recently been sunk; the water is good and very cold. Though there may not be very much of the town of Phellos above ground these days, it is worth it just to take in all the incredible beauty of the surrounding area. With its green vegetation and fresh air, Phellos is close enough from Kaş to reach on foot.

A house-type Lycian tomb in Phellos.

Kaş - Antiphellos

One of the fastest expanding towns in the field of tourism is Kaş. As the town was established over the ancient city of Antiphellos, in Middle Lycia, there are not many ruins that remain above ground. An inscription found in Kaş written in two languages definitively establishes the fact that the city lying under Kaş is Antiphellos. However, the original name of Kaş was Habesos or Habesa in the ancient tongue of Lycia, whereas it was later given the name Antiphellos.

Antiphellos was a small settlement area in the 4th century B.C. and was the harbor for Phellos, which was situated just above it. However, near the start of the Hellenistic period, Phellos contracted in size, whereas Antiphellos grew in size and importance. This situation continued through the Roman period, whereas cedar forest products and a flourishing sponge business brought in enormous riches to the city, diminishing the dependency on Phellos.

On the rise was probably the city's acropolis, one can see fortifications on the side facing Meis Island (ancient 'Kastellorizon'). However, no remnants of these fortifications are to be seen on the northern or western slopes. Ruins of a wall on the shoreline can still be seen today. To the west of the modern town, to the right of the road leading out to Çukurbağ Peninsula, stands the ancient theater of Antiphellos overlooking the sea. The fine masonry of this theater is quite attractive and was constructed of local limestone. This Hellenistic theater, which is remarkably intact today, once held 4,000 people who sat in 26 seating rows. Its tribunes and outer walls are still visible today, although no trace of the skene remains.

From the harbor, a path leads up to the west and very soon brings the visitor to the ruins of a small temple on the left. Only the lower parts are preserved, to a maximum height of five layers of ashlar blocks; the blocks are slightly bossed and in some cases have drafted edges. A vertical line, clearly distinguishable on the east side, where the blocks do not overlap, shows that the retaining wall was later extended or repaired. The original building dates back to the 1st

A Lycian sarcophagus lies sandwiched between picturesque homes in the market.

A panoramic view of the district of Kaş.

century B.C., the extension probably to the late third century A.D. The 450-meter breakwater, which belongs to the Hellenistic period, was used until recently, whereas it has lost its old condition through additions that have been made to it in later years.

Above the theater lies a house-type rock-tomb known as the Doric Tomb, and its form is unique. Cut from the sheer rock face in the shape of a slightly tapering cube some 4.5 m high by 4.5 m wide, with a passage all around, it stands complete apart from some damage at the top. There is a molding at the base and a shallow pilaster at each corner; all the capitals but one are lost. On the south side a band with mutules is preserved. The entrance, originally closed by a sliding door, has a molded frame surrounding an aperture 1.90 meters high. The interior consists of a single chamber; the bench at the back is decorated with a frieze of small dancing figures holding hands, seventeen on the bench itself and four on each return, and floral designs at the sides. The tomb probably dates to the 4th century B.C.

In the hillside to the north of the town are a number of rock-tombs, some at least quite easily accessible. One of these is interesting as having an upper story of Gothic-arch form and a Lycian

Modern structures and historical dwellings exist side by side in Kaş.

What the historical harbor of Kaş looks like today.

inscription to which has been added, centuries later, another in Latin when the tomb was re-used by a certain Claudia Recepta. Most of the tombs in Antiphellos, as elsewhere, are sarcophagi. In 1842, Spratt counted over a hundred, but the majority of these have been destroyed by the local inhabitants, who use the flat sides as building-stones; the curved lids, being less useful for this purpose, may often be seen lying alone.

One of these, however, is remarkable both for its elegant form and its excellent preservation. It stands at the upper end of Uzun Çarşı Caddesi, amongst the carpet shops and consists of three parts. The hyposorium is about 1.5 meters high, with a sunken floor; the door is broken open. Above this is a plain base about 80 centimeters high, these two parts being cut from the solid rock. On top is the sarcophagus itself, cut from a separate piece of stone, with Gothic lid and crest; from each side of the lid project two lions' heads resting on the paws. The short end of the lid is divided into four panels; in the upper two are standing figures in relief. On the hyposorium is a long Lycian inscription, written in a form of the language that has only been found on the Xanthos Obelisk, which has yet to be deciphered. As it hasn't been deciphered yet, nobody knows who it belonged to, whereas the local

97

Walls that show the fine masonry of the 1st century B.C. temple next to the Kaş Amphitheater.   *Lycian tombs situated on the hills above Kaş.*

people call it the King's Sarcophagus.

In addition to the historical artifacts, Kaş, which is the closest point to Meis Island, is a complete natural paradise. Stretching out into the sea like a tongue, one can see all the modern hotel development that has occurred on the Çukurbağ Peninsula. The peninsula also has a three-kilometer long nature track. One can also relax in the sparkling clean surf at choice beaches such as Büyük Çakıl, Küçük Çakıl and Akçagerme, all within the town limits of Kaş. In addition, one can go out to Çayağzı Beach by small motorboat. Of the six caves near Kaş, the most famous ones are Güvercinlik Cave (for its pigeons), Deniz Cave on Aşırlı Island, and Mavi Cave, which is

An aerial view of the Kaş Amphitheater.   *The Belly Dancer's Tomb (c. 4th century B.C.) located to the north of the Kaş Amphitheater.*

18 kilometers outside of Kaş. In the meanwhile, Kaputaş Beach is just out of this world.

In addition to the abundance of history found around Kaş, the town also offers numerous opportunities to take up sports in natural surroundings, such as trekking, mountain climbing and rafting. For those that wish to be left alone with nature, the natural choice is to check out Yeşil Lake and Uçansu Waterfalls, both of which are found in Gömbe. Gömbe is at the bottom of Akdağ, 70 kilometers outside Kaş. After the Kızlar Point, Akdağ is the highest summit in the Western Taurus Mountains. The small lakes found here are nature's spellbinding parts. There is the ancient city of

99

A panoramic view of Kaş.

The Büyük Çakıl (Big Pebble) Beach holds the spellbinding blue water of Kaş

·Chomba in Gömbe, where at a distance of 13 kilometers from here lies the ancient city of Nisa in Meryemlik, near Sütleğen. One can encounter tombs, an agora and ruins of a theater. The ancient town of Candyba is situated near the town.

A characteristic of Kaş is that some of the nearby ruins can be reached on foot. For instance, the 12 kilometers on foot from Kaş to Phellos would be a nice walkabout. The Phellos ruins are just above the villages of Çukurbağ and Pınarbaşı.

One should not arrive in Kaş without visiting Kekova. Just as one can get there from Kaş by boat,

you can also go overland to Üçağız and row out from there. It is just not possible, to see this wonder of the world and not be amazed by the sunken city. Just as there are a number of sites near Kaş, such as Istlada, Apollonia, Isinda, Cyaenai, there are also several sites whose names are unknown. As a consequence, it is possible to see artifacts on the side of the road or on the slopes of a mountain. For instance, there is an antique city in the village of Bayındır, seven kilometers outside Kaş. On the slopes above Bayındır Harbor, which is ideal for yachts to drop anchor, one can encounter a number of sarcophagi, one of which

is Lycian. There must have been a very small city of antiquity here, the name of which is thought to have been Sebeda.

On the high ground to the west of Kaş there are a number of ancient sites, though none of any great size. The most considerable is scattered about on the plateau of Seyret, overlooking a long valley down which a stream runs to join Felen River. The site, about 760 meters above sea-level, occupies three small hilltops and has a wall of unbossed polygonal masonry of apparently early date; the whole is comparable in extent with the site at Bayındır Harbor. Near the village of Sidek is a rocky eminence with a polygonal wall, an enormous Gothic sarcophagus, and a rock-tomb with a Lycian inscription.

Further to the north, above the scattered village of Hacıoğlan, on a hill about 600 meters above sea-level on the north side of the stream, is a walled area some 15 meters in length, a fort rather than a city. On the slope towards the stream are three Lycian pillar-tombs; one of them has a diagonal slot in the upper surface, but not large enough for a grave.

There is a town whose name is unknown, half an hour south of Bağlıca, near the village of Çardaklı, that has a fortress on the top of a hill. There is a small settlement known as Tysse on top of a low hill in the vicinity of the village of Tüse. Nearby, in a place called Aladam one can find a rather interesting Lycian tomb that has steps on its upper part.

The whole of this upland region, even in midsummer, is delightfully cool and green.

In the meanwhile, I'd like to acknowledge a debt of gratitude to the memory of the Late Prof. Dr. George Bean, who spent much of his life in Turkey wandering into every nook and cranny and who wrote a series of books concerning the ancient civilizations of Anatolia.

A view from Kekova, which can be reached from Kaş by both sea and overland.

Isinda

Like most Lycian cities, Isinda was founded on a rocky slope. It is situated near the village of Belenli, which is reached by exiting the Kaş-Finike road at Ağullu, 8 kilometers outside of Kaş. The ruins are a short walk from Belenli, and lie to the west of the village. You can take some of the volunteer village kids along for your walkabout.

Isinda was rather obscure and was practically never mentioned in antiquity. Like Apollonia, it is identified by inscriptions naming 'Aperlites from Isinda' found on the site and in the neighborhood.

The ring-wall, quite well preserved in part, is of poor-quality masonry and much repaired. At the highest point is the foundation of a building like a stoa, with steps on the long side and projecting wings at each end. Near the top of the hill are two house-tombs with Lycian inscriptions. At least two cisterns are to be seen, and on the slope towards the village a number of Gothic sarcophagi with Greek inscriptions.

The inclusion of Isinda in the sympolity with Aperlae is surprising, not so much for the distance, which is hardly greater than that between Aperlae and Simena, but because it lies in a quite different region, with the intervening mass of Mt. Kıran, 700 meters high. An association with Phellos would appear more natural.

Not far from Belenli is an unusual Lycian tomb, which is half house-tomb, half sarcophagus. The place is known as Çindam, 'the Chinese house', the name apparently applying to the tomb.

A view of the Isinda Necropolis.

Apollonia

Apollonia, like others of the minor inland towns of Lycia, was not mentioned at all by any ancient writer, unless we may suppose that Stephanus' notice of an island off the coast of Lycia, otherwise unknown; is an error for the city in question. The site is proved by inscriptions on the spot mentioning not only 'Aperlites from Apollonia' but also dedications to Augustus and Tiberius by the inhabitants of Apollonia.

The latter, made independently of Aperlae, suggest that Apollonia was not at that time merely a minor member of the sympolity, but an independent city; similarly, federal coins (very rare) inscribed APO, which can only be of Apollonia, cannot have been struck except by an independent city. Either, then, the sympolity did not exist until the time of the empire, or Apollonia was not an original member. The ancient settlement is thought to have dated to the 4th century B.C., like the other Lycian cities.

The ruins are on an 'L' shaped hill some 100 meters high above the village of Sıcak, officially Kılınçlı. They are reached by exiting the Kaş-Finike road towards Kekova, 22 kilometers outside of Kaş.

The town-walls are well preserved on the west side, and there is a small walled area on the summit, a poorly preserved theater, a large vaulted reservoir, and numerous cisterns of the familiar bell shape. Tombs are, as usual, abundant, especially on the north slope towards the village, and are mostly of sarcophagus-type. There are, however, six Lycian pillar-tombs, all uninscribed, sufficient by themselves to prove the antiquity of the site, one Lycian rock-tomb with a Greek inscription. The name 'Apollonia' is of course Greek; what the

One of the pillar-tombs of Apollonia.

Lycian name may have been is unknown.

The acropolis is enclosed in dressed stone fortifications, which are well-preserved and visible from the sea. During the Byzantine period, an inner citadel was constructed within these fortifications, containing a square-planned Heroum. A Byzantine church can be seen west of the citadel and west of this is a small theater, very similar to a number of others in the region.

The theater contains ten tribunes, although no trace of the skene remains.

One of the most striking monuments on the acropolis is the polygonal Heroum and the rock-tomb, carved out of the local rock.

Traces of a bath are to be seen north of the theater and the acropolis also contains wells and cisterns sufficient to provide the settlement with a constant water supply.

Kekova

Kekova, where history and nature have come together as one, shelters incredible beauties. An easily accessible place where 'blue voyagers' can feel confident about dropping anchor, Kekova exhibits unbelievable beauty that is a part of history. In reaching Kekova by sea, one can rent a small motorboat from Kaş or Kale Çayağzı.

After departing Kaş, one sails past Uluburun and sets a course for Kekova, a spot that is practically paradise. One first encounters Sıcak Peninsula, where the ancient city of Aperlae is found. At the end of this peninsula are two islands, Toprak and Kara. Kekova Island stretches out from here and it is because of this island that the surrounding region is called Kekova. It is also called the 'Sunken City' as the historical buildings on Kekova Island sank in the water as a result of various earthquakes. Passing between the islands and arriving at Kekova, the safest place to anchor is off the village of Üçağız, which is a decent all-round harbor.

If you are arriving overland, you exit the Finike - Kaş Highway where the signpost says 'Kekova' whereby after driving 19 kilometers, you arrive in the natural wonder which is the village of Üçağız.

This is an area where history mingles with nature and today's lifestyle. There are a number of ancient cities situated very close to each other here, such as Aperlae on the Sıcak Quay, Simena, in the sunken city of Kaleköy, Theimussa, which is found on Üçağız, and Istlada, which sits above Gökkaya Cove. In addition to these cities along the coast, there are also Apollonia in Kılıçlı, as well as the ancient city of Tyberissos, in Çevreli on the road two kilometers outside Üçağız. Tyberissos stands on a hill overlooking the plain of Tirmisin at 365 meters above sea-level. At the foot of the mountain, and little above the level of the plain, is an attractive glade in which are a dozen or so Lycian sarcophagi and a number of pigeon-hole tombs. By their inscriptions,

Two different views of the ancient city of Simena, in Kaleköy.

they are dated to Hellenistic and Roman times.

The main site is on the two summits of the hill. The northern is the higher and was evidently the acropolis, while as for the southern hill, at its southern end, standing up to 1.5 meters in height, is a small church or chapel, little over 6 meters long, which has replaced a Doric temple. As usual, the majority of the tombs in Tyberissos are sarcophagi, but there are two rock-tombs of house-type, both with inscriptions in Lycian. One of these is near the top of the hill, at the head of a gully leading from the south-east, close to the plain of Tirmisin, and carries a relief of two figures, man and woman, the style suggesting a date around 400 B.C.

From Çevreli, if you go towards Kapaklı, you arrive at a place called Enişdibi, about four kilometers down the road. If you walk about the eastern part of this field, that is, the side facing the sea, you will have the opportunity to see the famous ancient city of Istlada. As the cities around here were small, a few of them merged to be represented as one entity in the Lycian League.

For instance; Aperlae, Simena, Apollonia and Isinda were a part of this sympolity. Two kilometers down the road from Çevreli, one reaches the unbelievable beauty of Kekova. This road ends in Üçağız, where one can rent a motorboat to take you out to the sunken city of Simena, on Kaleköy.

Theimussa

The actual shelter for yachts is Theimussa, or present day Üçağız, which is a landlocked bay surrounded by green hills. There is an overland route that leads here. Though the ruins of the ancient city of Theimussa are located here, very little is known of its history. One inscription indicates that it goes back to the 4th century B.C. Here, one mostly comes across the ruins of a necropolis, whereas on the coast of this village, one can also find a door with its door frame still intact. Also, one can find some ruins of a tower on top of a low lying rocky outcrop.

A house-type Lycian tomb which belonged to Kluwainimi, found in Üçağız.

Right behind the quay are a pair of tombs. The oldest sarcophagus dates from the 4th century B.C. and is shaped like a house. Over it is the nude portrait of a young man. The inscription tells us that it belongs to "Kluwanimi." The work is Roman and a later addition to the sarcophagus. To the east, just above the sea are several sarcophagi which seem to have been stacked on top of each other. The majority

of these tombs belong to either the Hellenistic or Roman periods. The inscriptions on the tombs indicate at the owners were citizens of either Cyaenai or Myra. Just as Simena, Apollonia, Isinda and Aperlae formed a sympolity in Kaleköy, Myra and Cyaenai also formed a sympolity in Theimussa, whereas one of those cities represented the sympolity in the Lycian League.

At the east end of the site is a delightful little rock-cut quay or landing-stage, unlike anything else in Lycia. It is some 9 meters in length and nine meters wide. The rock-walls are cut vertical and still show the chisel marks; the floor is leveled, but the seaward edge is only roughly shaped. At the east end are cuttings in the floor which at present make shallow pools; their original purpose is obscure. In the back is a gate leading through to a kind of sunken road which is little more than a natural cleft; above it on the landward side stands a tomb. The sill of the gate is about two meters from the ground, and it is not clear how it was approached; the sill is broken away, but the hinge-holes and bolt-sockets are still to be seen. Also in the back wall is a smaller aperture like a window. There are other tombs above the gate and at the east end of the quay, the latter approached by steps; in both cases the lids are lying askew.

The necropolis of the ancient city of Theimussa, situated in Üçağız.

A panoramic view of Kaleköy Village with a distinct sarcophagus in the middle of the sea, which has become the symbol of the village.

(Following pages)

Simena

A Lycian sarcophagus which is submerged in the sea.

The village of Kale was established on top of the ancient city of Simena. Here, ancient history and modern day life are intertwined. From inscriptions that have been found, we know that the history of the ancient city of Simena goes back to the 4th century B.C. If we go ashore via the jetty next to the sarcophagus on the seashore and climb up the hill behind the houses, we reach the castle of Simena. This castle was used during the Middle Ages. Higher up, just below the castle wall, stood a stoa attached to a temple; remains of both buildings were noticed in former times, but all that is seen now are a few blocks built into a late wall and a fragment of an inscription bearing the name of Callippus.

Inside the castle is a charming little theater, entirely rock-cut; it has only seven rows of seats and measures a mere 16 meters in diameter. It cannot have held much over 300 people, a fair indication of the very modest size of the city. This is the smallest theater to be found throughout Lycia. There are rock tombs scattered about west of the theater. Above the rock tombs is a Roman wall built of dressed stone and located on the wall are late-period embrasures, thus giving one a simultaneous glimpse of three periods. On the shore are the ruins of public baths whose inscription is still legible and reads *"A gift to Emperor Titus presented by the people and council of Aperlae as well as by the other cities of the League."*

To the north of the castle on the northern summit of the hill are many sarcophagi. Looking out from the castle towards Üçağız, it becomes clear how beautiful and safe a natural harbor this really is. However, bathers need to be wary of sea urchins.

Different views of the sunken city of Kekova.

Kekova Island

Kekova Island - Tersane Cove. The church apse found here collapsed in recent times.

Another view of the sunken city on the shores of Kekova Island.

Giving its name to the whole area, this long island stretches four miles before Kaleköy and is filled with historical ruins. At the southwestern end of the island is Tersane Bay where yachts may approach. On the southern side of the bay are traces of sunken shops whose rooms are still discernible today. Leaving the jetty, one encounters by the apse of a Byzantine church. Though the place is full of ruins, no excavations have been carried out on this island, so little is known about its history.

On the landward side of Kekova Island, one may see the ruins of a sunken city. Following the shore, we see that half of the houses are submerged and that the stairways descend into the water. The foundations of buildings and houses can also be seen in the sea.

Aperlae

Aperlae is located on the Sıcak Peninsula, near the Sıcak Quay. One can easily reach here by renting a motorboat from either Kaş or Üçağız. If you are arriving overland, you may reach here from Apollonia, which is located in Kılıçlı. Aperlae's history, which dates back to the 4th or 5th century

B.C., is known from coins bearing its name. Aperlae was the head of the Aperlite sympolity, of which Simena, Isinda and Apollonia were also members, the four together presumably carrying one vote in the League assembly. How early this arrangement was is uncertain; Apollonia at least seems a very doubtful member in pre-Roman times. Citizens of the three associated cities were called officially in the inscriptions 'Aperlite from Simena', etc, and their own ethnics were not used.

The city walls begin at the shoreline and are fortified with towers at regular intervals. These walls, with their rectangular and polygonal construction, are from Roman times. Other remains at Aperlae are all from the Byzantine and Ottoman periods. The western reaches of the wall are of rectangular construction. There are three gates in this wall, two of which have a plain and the third, a blind archway.

The southern reaches of the walls are of polygonal construction and in a bad state of repair. This side is reinforced with two towers and it is here that the main gate was located.

Besides a church in the northwest corner and a chapel in the southeast corner, no other clearly defined structures can be found. Outside the early wall, especially on its east side, are numerous tombs, nearly all sarcophagi with rounded crest and lid. Some of them stand between the early wall and the shore, confirming that this area belongs only to the later fortified city. Today, one will find that the quay and associated structures of Aperlae are all underwater. Towards the west end a pier projected outwards.

Istlada

In the Lycian region, there is the small but rather impressive ancient city of Istlada. The four-kilometer road that splits off towards the east from the village of Davazlar on the Finike-Kaş Highway takes us up to the famous monument tomb at the Hoyran location in the village of Kapaklı. Here, across from the elementary school, is the so-called 'Hoyran' tomb with reliefs from the 4th century B.C.

At the highest point to the west is the fortified acropolis; on its east slope are two rock-cut tombs of house-type. One of these is highly unusual; it is cut from the rock so as to show the front and one side of the 'house', the side wall decorated with reliefs. At the north end of the village is another striking tomb, cut from an outcrop of rock; it too is of the house-type, but above the row of round beam-ends is a broad frieze adorned with reliefs. In the middle is a man reclining on a couch; in front of him a table and four armed men; behind him two male and six female figures. The pediment above is rounded and carries three more figures. All the persons but the first are standing. Over the door is a worn and broken Lycian inscription.

One can go by car to the end of the village. Parking your car next to the house-type tomb seen on the hill, you can first check out the tombs on the hill and then you can walk down a footpath to see the ruins on the opposite hill. Following this path, we can see the rock tombs behind the crop fields. From here, let's visit the first hill, where one can see nine sarcophagi bunched together in one spot. From here, a second hill that has been surrounded by a small fort. To the east and north directions of the acropolis, one can encounter tombs in the form of rock-tombs, sarcophagi, and stele. All of the tombs belong to the Roman Period. Behind these sarcophagi are Lycian house-type tombs that have been carved out of the living rock. One of these house-type tombs is known as the 'Pigeon' Tomb. Reliefs of a rooster, sphinx and a pigeon are depicted on the tomb. On the north side of this 4th century B.C. tomb is a frieze that depicts

Hoyran Monument
(c. 4th century B.C.)
Examples of different types of tombs in Istlada.

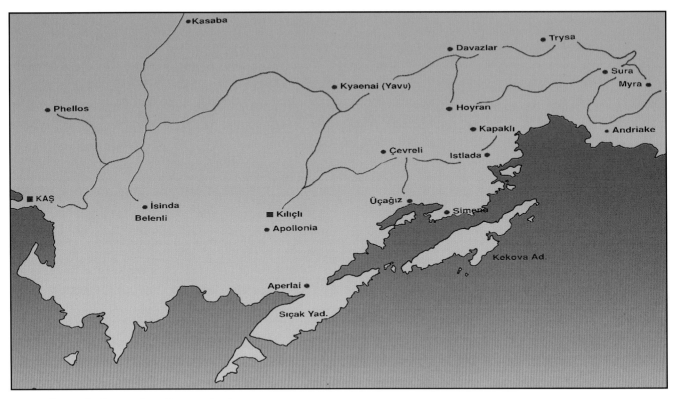

Nautical map of Kekova and neighboring inland Lycian cities.

An aerial view of Gökkaya Cove, which was the harbor of Istlada.

the tomb's owner and his relatives.

There are also ruins in the lower part of this section called Hoyran. If you are traveling by car, you need to arrive from the Kekova Road. Come down the Kekova Road and exit onto the Çevreli - Kapaklı Road, two kilometers before Üçağız. Drive along this road for 1.5 kilometers and you will encounter a fabulous Lycian rock-tomb in a place called Bucak. Here, you can see a 4th century B.C. tomb which has two people in relief sitting on top.

If you continue from here, and stop in a place called Enişdibi, before arriving in Kapaklı, you will again encounter ruins on the side facing the sea. If we park our car here and trek along the footpath, you shall reach some interesting ruins which are situated above Gökkaya Cove, not far from a place called

Hayıtlı. Here, one sees sarcophagi and architectural structures together, whereas the houses are intact up to their door stones. Next to these structures, one can see a part of a church apse still standing. Thus, here it is possible to see Lycian, Hellenistic, Roman and Byzantine period structures next to each other.

George Bean has mentioned that the name 'Istlada' could be read in the inscriptions written on the sarcophagi found here. Like the other small Lycian cities in the Istlada region, such as Apollonia, Aperlae and Phellos, there was one gentleman who practically ran the city himself. If the site above Gökkaya Cove is actually Istlada, then there must be some place that connects this site with the part where sarcophagi are situated in Hoyran. But in fact, there does not appear to be any sort of independent city in the vicinity. As a consequence, the works of Istlada

are scattered throughout Kapaklı, as well as Hoyran and Hayıtlı. From here, looking out over Gökkaya Cove and Kekova is certain to put you in a relaxing trance. In addition, it is very easy to get up here from the sea and Gökkaya Cove if you follow the path leading up from the church ruins at the back of the cove.

Overlooking the plain of Tirmisin on a hill standing 365 meters above sea-level and situated a few kilometers northeast of Üçağız, is the little-known city of Tyberissos. At the foot of the hill, and a little above the level of the plain, is an attractive glade in which there are a dozen or so Lycian sarcophagi and a number of pigeon-hole tombs. Other than the tombs, this site doesn't offer much else in the way of ruins, whereas it is not really worth the time for an extended visit.

A monument tomb found in a place called Bucak on the Kapaklı Road.

Cyaenai

Another place of ruins off the Kaş-Finike Road is Cyaenai, which is situated on a steep rocky slope above the village of Yavu, 23 kilometers from Kaş. One can drive up to the theater, and from there trek 45 minutes from the village over a rocky path. Cyaenai is another of the Lycian cities with a Greek name; like Xanthos, that of the color of dark blue. Cyaenai is also the name of the Symplegades, the Clashing Rocks, at the northern entrance to the Bosphorus.

We don't know exactly when this city was established, but judging from existing inscriptions we are able to date it as far back as the 4th century B.C., whereas Cyaenai was continuously inhabited since that time. The longest of these inscriptions is concerned with the honors decreed to a citizen named Jason, son of Nicostratus, a contemporary of Opramoas of Rhodiapolis and like him, generous with gifts of money to various cities; as many as 16 of the Lycian cities issued honorific decrees for him at different times. It is for these reasons that Jason held the title of Lyciarch. The town grew very prosperous during the Roman period, and was the center of a Bishopric during the Byzantine era, before being abandoned in the 10th century, with no trace of settlement beyond this date.

The town is situated on a steep hill rising some 290 meters from the little plain of Yavu; the climb to the summit takes 45 minutes, the present path follows the ancient one part way up. The top of the hill was surrounded by a wall on three sides enclosing an area some 450 meters in length and breadth. As it stands the wall is late, of poor, irregular masonry with many re-used blocks; but the original wall, well built in more or less regular bossed ashlar, is visible in its lower parts on the north and west sides. Three gates, also on the north and west, are still to be seen, and a fourth must be supposed at the south end of the west wall, where an ancient road entered the city.

The theater rests on the southern slope of the acropolis. The central section of the auditorium still stands, containing 25 rows. The uppermost level of the lower diazoma contains framed seats. It was probably built in the 2nd century A.D. and looks out over Trysa, Apollonia, with a fine view of the islands and bays of the coastline.

Between the acropolis and theater lies the necropolis, containing a large number of tombs of all sizes dating to the Roman period. Cyaenai holds the most sarcophagi throughout Lycia. For this reason this place is called 'City of Sarcophagi.' The ones on

A view of two different sarcophagi in Cyaenai. (below)

The Cyaenai Amphitheater, which dates to the Roman Age.

A view of sarcophagi, from Cyaenai, the City of Sarcophagi.

Various views of Cyaenai.

the west side are plain, while the ones on the eastern slope are varied and some of them have reliefs. These sarcophagi with reliefs date back to about 350 B.C. All the rest of the sarcophagi belong to the Roman period. In the lower part of the city, one encounters a very impressive tomb community that belongs to the Early Period. These are on both sides of the ancient road. The rocks here were carved in the shape of ladders. Just south lies a vertical rock that was shaped in the form of a sarcophagus. This sarcophagus is decorated in heads of lions and reliefs. There are rock tombs, which were cut out of the living rock in the bottom part of this sarcophagus. Behind this group, a stele with four facades can be seen.

Next to the other side of the ancient road are a number of rock tombs, some of which have inscriptions in the Lycian language. The tomb near the top of the hillside can be seen from the valley but it is not easy to reach. It has the form of a temple-tomb in the Ionic order; unusually, the porch has a single column between pilasters, with a dentil frieze and pediment above. Its inscription, written in Greek over the door of the main chamber, refers to the upper and lower tombs and to the sarcophagus. The lower tomb is the main chamber itself. There is a deep cut above the pediment of the upper tomb whereas it is situated as though it is sitting on top of another tomb's pediment. The tomb is dated by the style of the script to the 3rd century B.C.

A relief of soldiers with spears dating from the Lycian period was taken from one of the rock tombs on this site and is seen in the Antalya Museum today. Although the library, baths and water cisterns have been clearly identified, several of the remains in Cyaenai are unknown.

Trysa

This site is remote and not easily accessible; it lies on a crest in the eastern part of the plateau near the village of Gölbaşı about six kilometers north-east of Cyaenai. Some of its monuments are among the earliest in Lycia.

The discovery of Trysa, and in particular of its remarkable heroum, was among the most exciting events in Lycian archaeology. For the present-day traveler, the site has lost much of its interest as its principal sculptures have been carried off to Vienna, but it still has quite a lot to offer. Trysa is not mentioned anywhere in ancient literature; the name is known only from the inscriptions. Coins of League type inscribed 'TR' may well be of Trysa; the alternative is Trebenna, away in the northeast corner of Lycia.

Most of the sarcophagi are plain, or have bosses in the form of busts or animals' heads; but one in particular is very handsomely decorated. On one side of the lid are two gorgons' heads with a lion between them, and above this a man in a chariot-and-four between crowns and masks; he is likely to be the owner of the tomb, the crowns implying that he was a city magistrate. On the other side of the lid are two oxen, or rather cows' heads, and on the short end dolphins and other fishes. There are further reliefs on the crest of the lid; on the left an enormous goose with a man on its back, on the right a galloping rider, and between these a number of men and women; unfortunately the figures are much worn and the scene is hard to interpret.

In another place is a rock-cut stele with the representation of a large dog; apparently the dog protects the grave as he once protected the house. Another relief, which also may be from a tomb, shows on ox, a boy, and a man in a long robe raising his right hand; it has been suggested that the ox is sacrificial and the man is a priest.

But the great glory of Trysa is, or was, undoubtedly the heroum. This stands at the north-east end of the site and consists of a sarcophagus, cut from the living rock, in the middle of an enclosure some 20 square meters. The wall, about three meters high, was covered on its inner face on all four sides of

A view of Trsya from the Heroum.

A drawing which reflects the original condition of the Trysa Heroum.

the enclosure, and on its outer face also on the south side, with a frieze in two horizontal bands representing scenes from mythology. Among these are episodes from 'The Iliad and the Odyssey', from the exploits of Theseus, from the Seven against Thebes, battles of Greeks and Amazons and of Centaurs and Lapithae, as well as many other figures of doubtful attribution. On the other side are battle scenes.

The bottom row of the inner surface of the friezes, on the wall where the door is, depicts a death scene, whereas the row on top explains about a wild boar hunt scene with the famous mythological Greek hero of Meleagros. His uncles die during this hunt whereas his mother caused him to die in a very unforgiving manner.

On the other side of the door, one finds Bellerophontes and a chariot pulled by four horses. The Bellerophontes legend has to do with the plume of natural gas that burns on its own at a place called Çıralı, near Olympos.

The reliefs related with Theseus on the east wall of the heroum continue along the length of the wall in two friezes. While he was on his way to Athens to be with his father, Theseus, the son of the King of Athens, killed all the giant and wild animals that blocked his way. He becomes the most famous hero of Greece by killing the terrible Minotaur on the island of Crete. In addition, one also finds another hero, that of Perseus, on these friezes. Among the heroic deeds of Perseus, who was the son of Zeus and Diana, was the cutting off the head of the Medusa.

On the western half of the north walls of both the upper and lower sarcophagi deal with the subject of abduction. As for the other half, one can see a hunting scene with the Centaurs on two friezes. On the west wall decorations of the upper and lower sarcophagi, one sees up to a certain point, eight scenes of besiege with a struggle against the Amazons, followed by a battle scene.

A sarcophagus which is found in Trysa.

After all we have explained, it is sad that all we have left here is a few rocks we are sitting on. Inside the garden next and opposite the heroum are other tombs. The incredibly beautiful view of the heroum from here ushers us away from our sadness, even only for a little while.

The ruins extend over an area more than 550 meters in length, partly terraced and enclosed on the north and west by a wall of irregular masonry, patched in places, but not later than the 5th century B.C. On the other sides, the wall has disappeared. On the high ground at the west end stood a pillar-tomb, now overthrown and broken, but originally standing some 4 meters high and 1.25 square meters in area. The grave-chamber is at the top as usual; below it ran a frieze of warriors and horses, most of which is lost. Standing around are sarcophagi of later date.

The only recognizable ruins of the large temple situated in the western point are a few columns which have survived. Numerous pieces were found on the spot of an inscription honoring a citizen who served as priest of Zeus and Helios; we believe it belongs to the Sun God, Helios as this was Lycia, the land of sun and light.

Otherwise, apart from a number of cisterns, all the monuments are sepulchral. Most of the sarcophagi are plain, or have bosses in the form of busts or animals' head; but one in particular is very handsomely decorated. On one side of the lid are two gorgon heads with a lion between them.

The temple may accordingly have been dedicated to one or both of these deities.

A sarcophagus belonging to the sons of Parnos, Deremis and Aischylos, which shows a relief depicting a war chariot, dates back to 380 B.C. and is in the Vienna Museum. Another sarcophagus that was taken from Trysa belongs to the 2nd century B.C. and is currently in the Istanbul Museum of Archaeology.

Myra

One can easily reach the famous ancient city of Myra, which is situated in Antalya's district of Kale, 24 kilometers outside Finike, on the Kaş-Finike coast road. Myra retained her fame throughout the Middle Ages as the see of the servant of God, St. Nicholas, who spouted forth myrrh, in accordance with the city's name. Myra was established on the seaward cliffs of the mountains surrounding the plain of Demre from the northwest. At first, the city was established on top of the hill where the rock tombs are, then later on, it expanded by moving down below where it became one of the six important cities of Lycia. The city's first coins, which were minted in the 4th century B.C., depicted the figure of a mother god.

Rather surprisingly, there is no literary mention of Myra before the 1st century B.C.; but the surviving monuments and inscriptions leave no doubt of her importance from at least the fifth century. In 42 B.C., after the capture of Xanthos, Brutus sent his lieutenant Lentulus Spinther to collect money; the Myrans were reluctant and Spinther had to force an entry to the harbor at Andriace by breaking the chain which closed it. The Myrans then submitted and complied with his demands. The city was well treated by the emperors; in 18 A.D., Germanicus and his wife Agrippina paid it a visit and were honored with statues erected in the harbor of Andriace. In 60 A.D., St. Paul changed ships at Myra, that is, at Andriace, on his way to Rome. Myra's neighbor to the east was Limyra, and we learn from an inscription that there was a ferry service between the two.

Dignified by the title of metropolis, handsomely endowed by gifts of money from Opramoas of Rhodiapolis and Jason of Cyaenai, whereas the theater and its portico were constructed

A monument tomb which is found in Karabucak near Myra (Roman Age).

by Licinus Lanfus of Oenoanda, to whom 10,000 denars were donated for its completion. Myra was finally made the capital of Lycia during the time St. Nicholas was the bishop of Myra by Theodosius II (408-450). Myra and the church were demolished during the Arab raids in the 7th and 9th centuries, whereas the Church of St. Nicholas was totally razed to the ground during a naval assault conducted by the Arabs in 1034.

Two separate views of the Lycian house-type tombs which are situated next to the Myra Amphitheater.

As a result of the discomfort caused by the Arab raids, the frequent flooding over of the banks of the Myros Stream in which some structures were filled with earth, along with earthquakes that hit the region, the city was abandoned whereas Myra was subsequently identified as being a village. When the Turks arrived in this area, they encountered a shrunken Myra.

There isn't much remaining on the acropolis, which is situated on the mountain above the theater. Spratt, who visited Myra in 1842, stated that besides some small rocks nothing else remained on the acropolis.

The city walls, from the Roman Age has some wall remains that date to the Hellenistic Age and in fact even as far back as the 5th century B.C. Near the theater as you go towards the city, you will come across some later period ruins on the left side of the road that could be either baths or a basilica.

Myra's water needs were met through aqueducts that opened onto the rock face on the side of the valley where the Demre Stream flowed. It is possible to see these aqueducts today. The other structures of Myra are buried underground and are waiting for the time when they see daylight again. While arriving in Myra, one will notice a well-preserved Roman period monument tomb at a place called Karabucak above the road.

Andriace, which is the harbor of Myra at the mouth of the stream, was known as a famous soothsaying center, whereas there is also the ancient city of Trebenda, which is in Gürses, a few kilometers outside Sura.

Now beginning from the theater, let's get acquainted with the rock-tombs and the Church of St. Nicholas:

134

The Theater

The theater is large, some 115 meters in diameter, and of the Roman type. The vertical rock-face could not be utilized for the slope of the cavea, which is accordingly wholly built up. The building has recently been cleared and its appearance much improved; the general state of preservation is good. The cavea has a single diazoma with 29 rows of seats below it and six above, with fourteen stairways; it is surrounded by two concentric vaulted galleries, of which the outer gallery was in two stories. In the west gallery, on the wall between the two corridors, is an inscription reading 'place of the huckster Gelasius'; we may imagine him at his stall purveying the ancient equivalent of peanuts and ice-cream to the spectators as they flocked in. The diazoma is broad and backed by a 1.90 meter-high wall the point of which has a projection with steps on either side giving access to the upper seats. On the front of the projection is a figure of Tyche, with the inscription; "Fortune of the city, be ever victorious, with good luck." Fragments of the decoration, including broken columns and carved blocks, are lying on the ground. In the orchestra is an interesting inscription concerning imports and exports at Myra, requiring the city to pay to the League Treasury 7,000 denars annually out of the revenues from the import duty. The theater was destroyed as a result of an earthquake in 141 A.D. whereas the theater and its portico were re-constructed by Licinus Lanfus of Oenoanda, to whom 10,000 denars were donated for its completion. The theater was used as an arena later on, which was the reason why some alterations were made.

Reliefs on a tomb next to the Myra Amphitheater.

The Myra Amphitheater dates back to the Roman Age.

Rock Tombs

The famous rock-tombs of Myra are in two main groups, one above the theater and the other in a place called the river necropolis on the east side.

Just to the west of the theater the steep cliff is honeycombed with closely packed tombs of greatly varying form and size, though the majority are as usual of house-type. Many of them are quite elaborate, and some are decorated with reliefs in color. A few are of temple-type. Again, one can see steps carved out of the rock that lead to the temples.

The tomb found at the level of the theater orchestra is of house-type with a pediment in which are two warriors carrying shields and moving to the left; the man on the right appears to be grasping the other's shield as if to tear it from him.

In the middle of the group, about half-way up, are two tombs one above the other, with a third at the side; over the upper tomb is a more elaborate relief showing a man reclining on a couch, with his wife sitting beside him and three armed men, apparently his sons, standing to the left; smaller figures carrying a bowl and a double flute approach the bed from the left. The most interesting inscription is found on the tomb next to the theater, in which it reads, "Moschus loves Philiste, daughter of Demetrius."

After sufficiently inspecting these tombs, let us check out the tombs on the eastern face of the hill, that is, the place that is called the river necropolis on the east side. The tombs here resemble those next to the theater. Not very much above ground-level, and approached by a somewhat uncomfortable rock-path, is the monument known as the Painted Tomb, certainly one of the most striking throughout Lycia.

It is of the usual house-type and has in the interior a bench on the right and left sides; in front is a leveled platform with steps leading up on one side. But the outstanding feature is the group of eleven life-size figures in relief. In the porch on the spectator's

Myra's east necropolis, which hold the finest examples of Lycian house-type tombs.

left is the reclining figure of a bearded man raising a wine-cup in his right hand, evidently the father of the family, and on the opposite wall a seated woman, presumably his wife, with her children on either side of her.

On the smoothed rock-face outside the porch there stands on the left a tall commanding figure, apparently the same as the reclining figure, but dressed for outdoors with cloak and a long staff in his right hand. On the rocks to the right are five more figures: first a tall female raising her veil, similarly no doubt identical with the seated woman in the porch; her daughter stands beside her holding her hand. In addition to the family, servants are also depicted in the tomb. The identification of this scene is not entirely clear, but it appears that the figures in the porch represent the family's indoor life, while those on the rocks outside show them issuing forth from the house.

The three on the extreme right must then depict a separate scene. At all events it is clear that there is no question of a family visit to the tomb; the monument as a whole represents not a tomb but the family dwelling. The colors, which Fellows saw as red, blue, yellow, and purple, have now nearly disappeared, apart from a red and blue background to the reclining man. Higher up in the eastern group is a tomb with a pediment showing a lion savaging a bull; in the porch inside is a scene, including eight figures, somewhat similar to that on the Painted Tomb.

Two separate views of house-type Lycian tombs in Myra (4th century B.C.).

A view of the western necropolis next to the Myra Amphitheater.

140

Saint Nicholas (Santa Claus)

Geometrically-configured mosaics that decorate the floor of the Church of Saint Nicholas.

An icon of St. Nicholas which is on display in the Antalya Museum.

Saint Nicholas, who is known throughout the world as Santa Claus, was born in Patara, which was an important Lycian city along Turkey's Mediterranean coast.

Towards the year 300 A.D., a rich wheat trader who lived in the wealthy city of Patara had a son whom he named Nicholas. It is said that he came to Earth as a savior of the poor, that he was a present of the sky upon his birth, a fruit of a sacrifice and an answer to his mother's and father's prayers. While still a young man his exceptional nature was equally manifest; when a church in the course of building collapsed and buried him, upon his mother's lamentations the stones fell apart and he emerged unscathed.

Some time later, his father died, leaving him a substantial inheritance, whereby Nicholas decided to spend the wealth to help the poor and needy. It is said that when he heard of a distinguished citizen of Patara who had fallen into penury and was unable to find dowries for his three daughters, Nicholas decided to help them. He went to the girls' house at night in order not to attract so much attention and also not to hurt anyone's pride. While they were asleep, he threw a sack of gold through the open window of the oldest girl. She found the money in the morning, whereby she was subsequently saved from her bad situation.

Later on, Nicholas wished to put up the dowry money for the other two girls, but because their windows were closed, he threw the bags of gold down the chimney, hence the secret bestowal of presents to children at Christmas.

Here is a story related to the life of St. Nicholas;

Nicholas travels to Jerusalem on a pilgrimage. On the return voyage, he saves the ship from sinking

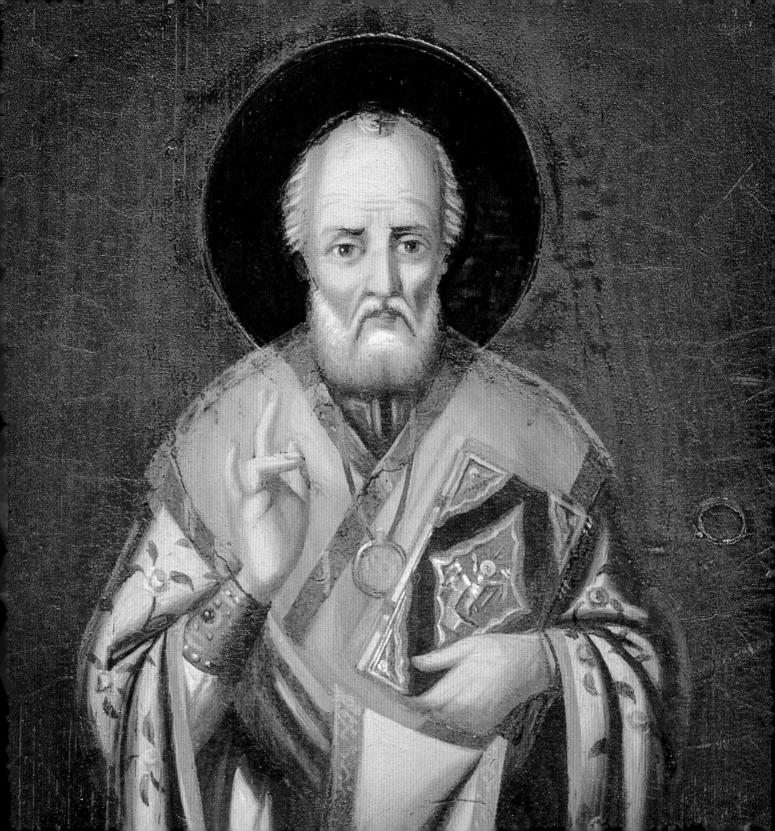

through prayers, whereas he even resurrected a sailor who had fallen off the ship and drown in the sea. Ever since that day, St. Nicholas has been accepted as the savior saint of sailors.

Some time later, Nicholas migrates from Patara to the neighboring city of Myra. Even his election as bishop of Myra was not without divine intervention; the dignitaries assembled in the church at Myra to make the choice were instructed by God to elect the man who should enter the building on the following morning. As St. Nicholas was the first to arrive at the church, he was selected to become Bishop. The miracles continued to occur here as he saved three generals from death. Another story about him goes as follows;

Once in a time of famine, a fleet of ships carrying corn from Alexandria to Byzantium called at Andriace; Nicholas, hurrying to the harbor, ordered the captains to surrender a hundred bushels from each ship, which they unwillingly did; when the fleet eventually arrived in the capital, the cargo was found to be still intact. The corn thus secured by the saint sufficed the Myrans miraculously for two years and still left enough for sowing.

Just like other Christians, Nicholas was thrown in jail for a period during the reign of Emperor Diocletianus and Licinius, both whom were against Christians. In the year 325 A.D., an assembly meeting was held in Nicaea (modern day Iznik) to solve problems dealing with Christianity, whereas Myra participated as Archbishop. The legend surrounding this event was how Nicholas restored three boys who while wandering about in this time of famine, found their way to the house of a butcher who murdered them in their sleep, cut up their bodies, and salted them in a tub, intending to use the flesh in the way of trade. Nicholas, informed of this occurrence by an angel, came to the butcher's house and restored the boys to life. This story was later claimed by a clergyman by the name of Bonaventure. It is believed that the savior of students, St. Nicholas died in Myra on December 6th, at the age of 65. In constructing a church in his name, the Myrans left him to rest in his sarcophagus for eternity. However, during one of the Latin Crusades, a band of men from Bari broke open the tomb and carried off some of the bones of the Saint to Italy on April 20, 1087 and buried them on

An interior view of the Church of St. Nicholas.

the grounds of a basilica they had built. Bones that are said to have remained from that raid are kept in the Antalya Museum.

The Church of Santa Claus

When the church or chapel that was erected for St. Nicholas collapsed in an earthquake in 529, a larger church or perhaps even a basilica-type church was constructed in its place. The architect Peschlow surmised that the two small spaces with equal-sized apses on the north side of the large apse as well as a major portion of the north side aisle in today's building belonged to this first structure. This church was re-constructed again after it was destroyed in the 8th century, due to either an earthquake or Arabian raids. The Church of St. Nicholas was totally razed to the ground during a naval assault conducted by the Arabs in 1034. An inscription records that it was restored under Constantine IX in 1043. Some additions were made to the church when it underwent renovation in the 12th century.

We understand that some repairs were made to the church and that the people worshipped freely in the church of Myra when the region was captured by the Turks in the 13th century. The chapel next to the big church was repaired in 1738. Ch. Texier, who explored Anatolia between 1833-37, passed through Myra and mentioned the church in his writings. Ten years later, in March, 1842, Lieutenant Spratt and Prof. Forbes arrived in Myra and drew up a plan of the church, whereas they mentioned that they saw a monastery next to the church.

During the Crimean War of 1853, the Russians took an interest in the church, whereas around the same period, the land on which the church stands is said to have been purchased by a Russian consul (other accounts say a Russian princess) with a view to reanimating the cult of the saint, but this was thwarted by the Sublime Porte, who upon realizing the political implications of the matter bought the land back and only authorized the restoration of the church. Thus, a Frenchman by the name of August Salzmann was given the task of renovating the Church of St. Nicholas in the year 1862. These restorations were conducted rather shoddily, whereas the original layout of the church was ruined. The belfry, which is seen today, was added during this restoration work, in 1876.

The St. Nicholas Statue located in the front garden of the Church of St. Nicholas.

There are close to 2,000 churches throughout the world dedicated to St. Nicholas, who is the savior saint of several cities. One can find his life story and miracles in a number of books, however the earliest description goes back to around 750-800 A.D., which was written by Brother Michael at the Stadium monastery in Byzantium.

Let's take a look together at the Church of St. Nicholas, which is an attractive example of Anatolian Byzantine architecture.

Walking past the entrance, one descends down a path of cut stone. While descending, we pass the statue of Santa Claus in the garden to our left.

Extensions on the north side as well as a chapel in the shape of a cross were added to the 4th century church, which had a single dome when it was first constructed. The church is in basilica form, with three aisles, to which a fourth has at some time been added on one side. In the apse at the end of the central aisle or nave is a synthronon with a covered passage running round and a stone placed as an alter. Inside the niche of the Apse are figurines of saints that have lost their color in places and are not so defined. The fresco in the small niche under these is that of St. Nicholas. One can see mosaic panels of different designs on the floor of this section as well as that of the southeast chapel in the actual church. On the west are a narthex and exonarthex, and pleasant cloisters on the north side. The walls contain re-used material including fragments of inscriptions. Within the niche opposite the stairs on the west side are frescoes of Jesus, Mary and John the Baptist.

From here, a well-preserved door frame takes us out into the section where the sarcophagi are found, that is, the long section of the cross-shaped chapel. Even if the frescoes inside the niches where the sarcophagi sit are not clearly defined, the chapel has been decorated with frescoes depicting various saints. An interesting example is that of the fresco of Mary, found above the columns of the north wall's first niche. From where the fresco of St. Nicholas is situated in the second niche, it is understood from the inscriptions that the column was placed upside-down.

Of the sarcophagi situated in the niches, it is accepted that the first one, which is a Roman Age sarcophagus, and is decorated with acanthus leaves, belonged to St. Nicholas. In fact, because St. Nicholas was the saint of seamen, it is said that the lid of the sarcophagus was decorated with fish-scale designs. A band of pirates from Bari broke open the sarcophagus and carried off some of the bones of the Saint to Italy on April 20th, 1087.

The sarcophagi found in the second niche as well as that in the opposite niche are plain. Besides

The sarcophagus of St. Nicholas.

A view of the Church of St. Nicholas.

HORREA IMP. CAESARIS DIVI TRAIANI PARTHICI ED IVI NERVA... ...EPOTIS TRAIANI HADRIANI AVGVSTI COS. III.

the sarcophagi found inside the niches here, there are two other tombs located elsewhere on the church grounds. From here, one passes through a door into the church courtyard, which is laid with thick blocks. There are two tombs in a niche of the courtyard that have long since been emptied out. Next to these are blocks of marble with cross and anchor motifs that must have been made for St. Nicholas.

The inscription found on the tomb situated inside the left wall dates back to the year 1118. Before entering the courtyard, one passes through the exonarthex, then through the narthex that opens into the synthronon. Here, one can see frescoes depicting the bishops in a group. The actual place, which is passed through here, opens out to side aisles with three belts. There are two aisles in the south of the synthronon. Even though it is said that the sarcophagus in the niche inside the second aisle is that of St. Nicholas, the man and woman relief on top of it indicates that this cannot be such. In the dome of the north aisle are frescoes of the Prophet Jesus and the 12 Apostles. To the side, one encounters an excavation of the side aisle. There are three rooms in the western part of the aisle where excavation is being carried out. In the middle of the building, a large diagonal ribbed vault erected from cut stone was used where there should have been a cupola with windows and a drum.

148

Andriace

*The ancient harbor of Andriace,
which has been transformed
into a marshy lake.*

Known as the port of Myra, Andriace is in Çayağzı, which is a five-minute drive from this ancient city. It can be reached from the Finike-Kaş Road via Sapag (past the Demre exit), by continuing for a few kilometers when one first arrives at Andriace and a few kilometers later at the harbor.

Although described as the port of Myra, Andriace was actually founded as a sister-town around the same time as Myra. It was taken in 197 B.C. by the fleet of Antiochus III along with the other Anatolian settlements in the hands of the Ptolemies at the time. Emperor Trajan had stated his plans to develop Myra as a port after visiting the area, but this plan was not realized until the reign of Hadrian.

The port itself was built close to the settlement of Demre at the entrance of the harbor. One of the most striking features of the site is the aqueduct system supplying the city with water. At the mouth of the harbor stands the remains of a monumental fountain dating to the Roman period. The agora, otherwise known as the 'Placoma' is the largest structure on the site. It is surrounded by shops on three sides with a large cistern in the center. A silo is situated to the west of the agora, whereas this 'granarium' was a building measuring 65 x 32 meters and containing seven separate grain storage chambers. These chambers were all internally linked but each one had a separate entrance on the facade. The guard rooms were positioned at the sides. The facade was covered with flat stones, whereas the side and rear walls were done in polygonal style. An inscription over the entrance and a relief of Hadrian and Empress Faustina in the center of the facade indicate that it dates to 129 A.D. The facade of this well-preserved building also contains a series of reliefs related to a dream of Heracleon, a state official in Andriace during the 5th century A.D.

Traces of vernacular dwellings and the harbor road are near the granary and next to these are semi-roofed quays. A defense tower can be seen on the west of the slope, and the necropolis lies to the north of the settlement. Here, one may see Lycian-type tombs of the Roman period, and two Byzantine churches, as well.

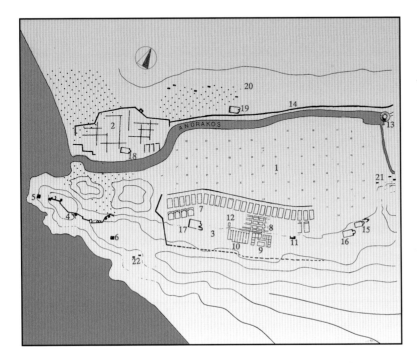

Sura

Sura lies to the west of Myra, an hour and a half on foot. It is located directly above the Andriace ruins in Çayağzı, whereas these days, the road to Kaş passes through the ancient town of Sura.

Sura was never an independent city, but merely a dependency of Myra; it is hardly mentioned except in connection with its fish-oracle, which, however, had considerable notoriety and is described in some detail in the ancient literature. At the extreme end of a plain some half a mile in length is the tiny 'acropolis' rising little more than 10 meters above the level of the plain, which was surrounded from the west by a thick wall. Placed at the ends of the walls were two adjacent chambers which opened out to a corridor in the center. The wall in the north formed into a rectangular-shaped tower, whereas the tower in the south has been reduced to rubble. A dozen or so Gothic sarcophagi are scattered about. On the hill is a rock-cut house-tomb with Lycian inscription, and at the southwest corner is a conspicuous statue-base with a very long Lycian inscription of which only a few letters of each line remain. On the south side is a row of rock-cut stele with lists of clergy attached to the cult of Apollo Surius.

But the chief interest of the site lies in the temple and oracle of Apollo. Immediately to the west of the acropolis the ground falls steeply for several hundred feet to the head of a marshy inlet. The temple stands close to the edge of the marsh; it is quite small and in fair preservation. Carved on its interior walls are a number of inscriptions recording devotions paid by suppliants; close by are the extensive ruins of a Byzantine church which has, as so often, succeeded the pagan temple and prolonged the sanctity of the place into medieval times.

A view of the Sura Necropolis.　　　　　*A view from the road of the Apollo Temple and a church, which are found below Sura.*

Just a few kilometers beyond Sura along the same road in the modern day town of Gürses is what is thought to be the ancient town of Trebenda.

There isn't much information about the name or history of this town, in which one encounters wall ruins and sarcophagi, whereas the great majority of the sarcophagi belong to the Roman Period.

There is a Lycian-type sarcophagus with relief figures that dates to the 5th century B.C. The acropolis is surrounded with walls from the east and west.

153

Limyra

The ruins of Limyra are nine kilometers away from Finike. The site is located in Torunlar, which is between Turunçova and Kumluca, at the foot of Tocat Mountain (1,216m) and can be seen from the road.

Known as 'Zemuri' in ancient times, Limyra was one of the oldest cities in Lycia of which we have proof of its existence back to the 5th century B.C. The city, with its rich and abundant soil, gradually became a prosperous trade settlement. Pericles adopted Limyra as the capital of the Lycian League to go up against the Persians, whereas the everlasting flame of Lycia was

A model of the Heroum built by the Limyran King Pericles in 370 B.C. What remains of the Heroum today.

symbolized here with a constantly burning torch. During the 4th and 5th centuries B.C., Lycia, as well as the rest of Anatolia, was under the administration of local governors called satraps, who were under the control of the Persian kingdom. Alexander the Great put an end to all that when he arrived on the scene in 333 B.C. Thus, the Limyra region, which was captured by Alexander, was subsequently administered by Governor Nearchus, Alexander's commander, whom was left in Lycia to govern in his absence. After Alexander's death, the Empire was divided between the neighboring states, and the region of Limyra was given first to Antigonos, and later to the Ptolemic dynasty of Egypt. It was captured in 301 B.C. by Lysimachus, after which for a period the Ptolemies dominated the area once more. Finally, it remained under Ptolemic control until 197 B.C., when the city of Limyra was taken over by King Attalos III, of Syria.

Subsequently, Limyra was handed over to Rhodes as a result of the Apemaia Treaty, which came about after the defeat of Antiochus at Magnesia. But the Lycians did not much care for Rhodian domination of Rome, whereas frequent riots that the Lycians caused were more than enough for Rome to constantly turn its attention to this region. Finally, in 167 B.C., the region was taken from the Rhodian Kingdom by the Romans, and included in the Roman Empire. Limyra, which had become a member of the Lycian League in the 2nd century B.C., was even in a position to strike its own coins. The period from the time Pericles died in the 1st century B.C. until the mid - 2nd century A.D. was considered the halcyon days of Limyra. However, the city was literally knocked off its feet by the earthquake which struck the area in 141 A.D. As a consequence, the town was reconstructed, thanks in large part through the patronage of the wealthy Opramoas, who from what we can determine

from his inscription, was also responsible for the construction of the theater.

During the Byzantine period, Limyra was a prosperous town once more, and in fact, became the center of a diocese. However, the city lost its importance and was abandoned soon after the Arab raids of the 9th century. Now, let's go through the ruins of this interesting city together, the site of which we encounter several monuments that have been excavated by Prof. Dr. J. Borchardt.

Climbing up a winding road to the top of the hill above the city and we encounter Limyra's acropolis, which is comprised of an inner fortress, or keep, to the north along with a lower fortress in the southern part which widens out into the shape of a triangle. There are surrounding battlements, cisterns and a Byzantine church in the lower fortress. Besides these, the most impressive remains are those of the Pericles Heroon. Situated near the southern walls, this mausoleum was carved from the natural rock face overlooking the plain of Limyra, measures 10.40 x 6.80 meters in size, and sits on a rock terrace that measures 19 x 18 meters. The Heroon of Limyra, which resembles the Nereids' Tomb in Xanthos, was constructed in 370 B.C. after the death of King Pericles, of Limyra, who worked tirelessly to establish the Lycian League.

The roof of the Heroon is held in place in the front and rear by caryatids. Today, many architectural fragments as well as reliefs of the monument are to be found in the Vienna Museum. The 5.3 meter high monument is in the form of a temple, and bearing friezes six meters in length. These friezes contained scenes of a war chariot pulled by four horses, followed by the King and his entourage, who were in turn followed by calvary and foot-soldiers at the rear, bearing spears in the right hand, and shields in the left. From the style of dress, it appears that these are Lycian and Persian soldiers.

Now let us look at Limyra's theater, which is at the side of the road. As we previously mentioned, the theater was destroyed in the big earthquake of 141 A.D., whereas it was rebuilt by wealthy Opramoas. The vaulted, double diazoma skene of this Roman theater has since fallen into ruin. Immediately opposite are remnants of fortifications of the Roman and Byzantine periods. These walls divide the site into two sections; the eastern one containing the ruins of a Byzantine church and a palace. This area is reached through an archway in the center of the northeastern wall, flanked on both sides by towers. In the western area, which also has an archway, is the cenotaph of Gaius Caesar, who was adopted by Augustos in 17 B.C., and

Catabura's Tomb in Limyra (c.350 B.C.).

House-type Lycian tombs found at the Çavdır Junction in Limyra (c. 4th century B.C.).

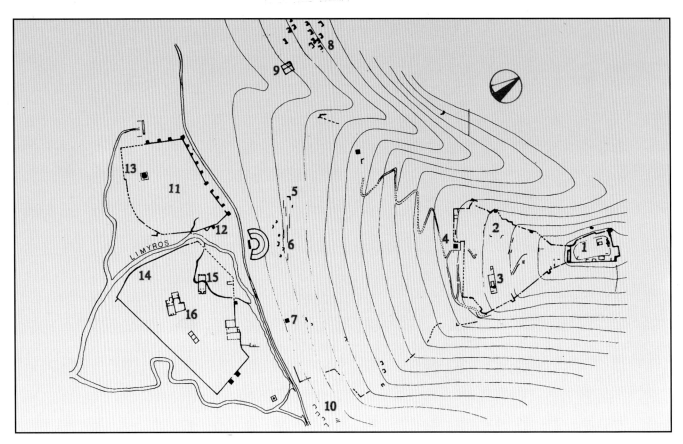

appointed to be his heir. Gaius Caesar was actually the son of Agrippa and Julia. When Gaius Caesar was maliciously wounded at a conference in Armenia and died at Limyra in 4 A.D., the Limyrians erected this monument over his tomb on behalf of his step-father Augustos. Subsequently, Limyra's relations with Rome were put on a good footing which culminated with Limyra's independence, whereas the state remained independent up to the mid-1st century A.D. Today, only the ruins of a wall in the shape of a tower can be seen of this tomb. It is understood that there is an explanation of Gaius Caesar's great deeds on top of the parts that were found of tomb. Nearby this monumental tomb lies the Ptolemy Monument from the following era. Only a very small part of this monument, which was decorated with acanthus leaves

and Egyptian influences and which had a wall that passed through it, can be seen today. The Byzantine wall that passed over the monument was revealed while research studies were being made on the statue of wife of Ptolemy.

The city wall makes a turn at the top, whereas one encounters Pericles Palace inside. It would be easier to reach this part if you pass between the walls. In addition, the city's avenue has remained underwater as a result of the stream flooding over, which has taken on a dramatic appearance.

The necropolis of Limyra is situated beyond the theater and is scattered over a wide area, roughly separated into the western, northern and eastern necropolis. The most noticeable tomb in the western necropolis is a two-tiered tomb, near which stands

Tomb of Gaius Caesar.

Ruins of the Ptolemy Monument's acroteria.

another interesting monument, the tomb of Tebursseli the portal of which is carved in relief. This tomb dates to the 4th century B.C. The relief carving shows Tebursseli and Susantre in battle with Arttumpara, King of Telmessos.

Situated above the theater one encounters the tomb of Catabura, who was most probably the brother or another relative of King Pericles of Limyra. From the inscription on the tomb, we learn that it was built around 350 B.C. The sarcophagus is mounted on an ornamented base, on which there are scenes of the traditional banquet of mourning, accompanied by an interesting relief of the judgment of the dead. The deceased is portrayed nude, with his clothes draped over his arm, appearing before the court in the world of the dead.

Tombs in Limyra's eastern necropolis.

Roma dönemine ait Limyra Tiyatrosu.

In the eastern necropolis, there is a monument tomb dating back to the 4th century B.C. with Ionic columns that were carved out of the rocks. There are also other tombs nearby, a number of which have reliefs depicting various scenes.

Not far from Limyra itself, there is quite an interesting tomb to be found on the banks of the Çavdır River which is decorated with reliefs of the family owners of the tomb; the father in one corner, with the mother and child in the other.

There are also a group of rock tombs to be seen in the vicinity, on the way to Elmalı from Finike, on the northeast side of the ride, close to the top of the hill. These tombs are interesting, as they seem to have been carved out of the rock to resemble medieval fortresses.

161

Arycanda

The site of the ancient settlement is located near a small hamlet called Aykırıçay, in the district of Arif, on the Elmalı-Finike Road.

We know this city went by the name Anna and was an Anatolian town around 2000 B.C.

However, through ancient works that have survived to this day, we are able take the existence of Arycanda as far back as the 5th century B.C. Like all the other Lycian cities, Arycanda, the name of which is locally derived, was invaded by the Persians in the 5th century B.C. It was annexed by Alexander the Great in 333 B.C. It remained under the rule of the Ptolemic Dynasty on his death, and was then taken by Antiochus III in 197 B.C. It was annexed to Rhodes as a result of the Apemaia Treaty and formed an independent league together with the other cities of Lycia, minting coins as a member of this league. The league lasted until 43 A.D., when it was disbanded by Emperor Claudius, whereas Arycanda was annexed to Rome, along with the rest of the region. It survived through the Byzantine era, when it became known as Acalanda, until the 9th century, when the settlement moved to a new site south of the modern road.

The site is extensive, stretching from the source of Aykırıçay Springs to the slopes of Şahinkaya, where it rises in terraces, densely-packed against the rock face. A stadium with one face can be seen on the uppermost terrace. Niches have been exposed behind the stadium's seating rows. The terrace that comes down from this stadium to the terrace below contains a well-preserved theater, with a small auditorium that rests on the natural slope of the hill. This structure, which had a Greek plan, was built in the Roman period. Greek inscription friezes can be seen lining the top two terraces of the 20-row auditorium.

On the terrace below rests the odeion of Arycanda, which was uncovered during excavations

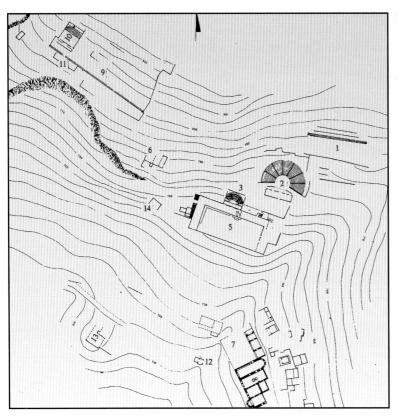

A panoramic view of the ruins of Arycanda.

A frontal look of an Arycanda tomb in the shape of a temple.

led by the Turkish archaeologist, Prof. Cevdet Bayburtluoğlu, who has been uncovering new artifacts every year. The odeion was exposed in 1978, whereas a section of it has been restored.

The main entrance to the odeion is to the south, through a triple portal. The interior was lined with orthosats, whereas it is understood that the walls used to be covered in colored marble. A frieze comprising of large blocks sits one meter above the outside face of the portals. Depictions of masks or gods are found in the center of each block. At the same time, a portrait of Hadrian is in the exact center of this frieze.

Behind the odeion are two opposing portals, whereas these portals opened out onto the ramp leading in front of the terrace wall of the theater in the eastern section. The west portal, opens onto the stepped way leading around the agora of the town. The odeion portico, which measures 75 x 8 meters, is decorated with floor mosaics. This portico turns back

Ruins which are still standing in Arycanda.

to the agora in a U-shape. Only a few of the shops in the eastern part of the agora can be made out today. On this flatland, which is embellished with a single tree, lies the remains of what was once Arycanda's state agora and in the vicinity where the tree is a structure that was most probably the agora shrine.

To the west of the theater and the agora on the upper terrace lies ruins of the bouleuterion, or what we would refer to today as the city hall, the tribunes of which are carved out of the rock face. A long stoa stretches beyond the front of this structure, whereas the site in front of the stoa is a cistern.

Between the bouleuterion and the agora is a small ruined bath and fountain, whereas the remains of a larger bath are found below the agora. From the surviving sections of the baths, it is plain that the eastern section was used as a terrace for it has an extraordinary view. Next to the baths stands a gymnasium, and to the west of that lies a house bearing inscriptions.

165

The Arycanda Amphitheater.

Ruins of the Roman Baths of Arycanda.

The necropolis on Arycanda's east side stretches over the terraces above the bath, while that on the west side stretches from the source of the Aykırıçay all the way to the cliffs just west of the city. The first structure one encounters in the necropolis on the east side is a mausoleum in the form of a temple with a podium. This mausoleum, with its 'in antis' plan and Corinthian order has left many people quite surprised, as they have made this structure out to be a temple.   A lion-figured relief decorates the facade, whereas an inscription on the tomb gives the name of the owner. The necropolis also contains a number of vaulted tombs and sarcophagi. The structure that sits to the east of the bath and the dwelling with an inscription is most probably a heroum.

One encounters just a few rock tombs in Arycanda, whereas most of these are located near the Aykırıçay Springs. Besides the rock tombs, here one can also see some rather interesting aqueducts that have been carved out of the rocks. We have ascertained from these aqueducts that Arycanda obtained its water from the Başgöz Springs. The aqueducts were connected to two large cisterns found to the west of the gymnasium. You can take an incredible photograph of all these ruins from the top of the surrounding mountains.

Olympos

In order to reach Olympos from the Antalya-Finike Highway, you need to turn off at the Ulupınar Road, where there is a signpost that indicates the ruins. This narrow road, which is surrounded by abundant natural beauty, descends all the way down to shores of Olympos. In order to reach the ruins from the parking lot, you cross the stream and after walking along the wide beach for some time, you will reach the banks of the stream which runs through Olympos. The path running along the banks of the stream leads up to the ruins. If perchance you have the time and you have got your swimsuit with you,

you shouldn't pass up the opportunity to go for a splash in the deep blue sea.

Olympos was established in the Hellenistic Age. In 100 B.C., Olympos became one of the six primary members of the Lycian League that were entitled to three votes. Coins were struck there in the 2nd century B.C. and during the 1st century B.C., it became a place where pirates, lead by Zenicetes, frequented quite often. This fearless pirate was finally defeated in 78 B.C. by the Roman Governor of Lycia, Publius Servilius Vatia, in an open-sea battle, after which Olympos and the surrounding area was merged to became a Roman province.

During the Roman period, the area became quite famous with the Hephaistos cult and their God of the Blacksmith where they worshipped at the site of the natural gas that spewed from the ground at nearby Çıralı..

During the 2nd century A.D., the man known throughout Lycia for his assistance and philanthropy, Opramoas from Rhodiapolis, made lavish gifts of money to Olympos to have many new buildings erected and old ones repaired. Thus, Olympos grew extremely prosperous during this century, but it was in the 3rd century that the pirates returned to annoy Olympos. The pirate raids were the reason this rich and flourishing city became impoverished overnight and lost its importance. From this point on, the city continued on as an insignificant small town.

It was used by Venetian and Genoese pirates for a period, during which time the harbor was enclosed by a wall built by the Genoese. When the

Plan of Olympos

1. Temple 2. Baths
3. Bridge 4. Acropolis
5. Church
6. Amphitheater
7. Middle Ages Fortress

Olympos is situated along a riverbank which empties into the Mediterranean Sea.

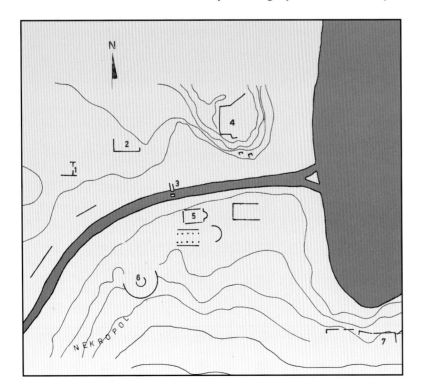

A view from the sea of Olympos, an ancient town that settled amongst the mountains.

pirates in the area were chased off by the Ottoman fleets, the city was abandoned in the 15th century.

Olympos was spread out over both sides of the stream that passed through it. Let's trek along the banks of the stream to wander around Olympos. The high hill, which can be seen from the shoreline, and which has a number of tombs, is the acropolis of Olympos. As for the structural remains on the hill, they belong to walls that were erected in the manner of a tower during the Middle Ages. When you look from the hilltop, you can take in the magnificent view of the river which looks oddly reminiscent of Venice. The stream was turned into a canal with walls that were built along the banks using a polygonal technique, whereas one can tell from traces that there

was a bridge that spanned both sides.

From the shoreline, the first thing we see as we enter the city beneath the acropolis are two tomb chambers. The tombs belong to the 2nd century, but were used for a second time in the 5th century. It wasn't until recently that the ruins behind the acropolis walls, which were turned into a tower in the Middle Ages, were brought to light. Through the excavation work of the Antalya Museum, a number of tombs were uncovered. We don't have too much information about the single sarcophagus that rests in the eastern part of the acropolis. Next to this is a burial chamber dating back to the 5th century A.D., that contains two sarcophagi which also has mosaics embedded in the floor of a soldier and a lion. The

sarcophagus that faces east was that of an Olympian named Marcus Aurelius Zosimas, whereas the one next to it belonged to the uncle of Zosimas, Captain Eudemos. On top of the captain's sarcophagus is a ship in relief along with an inscription that tells of the voyages made by Captain Eudemos to the Marmara and Black Seas. There is also a very emotional poem on the left side of this inscription, which is framed.

By moving on past these tombs a little bit, let's turn down a narrow road that goes by the right side of the second spring. There are a few ruins located on this side of the river. In this part, a monument tomb with two sarcophagi can be seen. Just a bit further ahead is another tomb. If we walk past these tombs towards the west, we will reach the bishop's house. This structure, which has been determined to be the house of the bishop, was built during the 5th century, whereas we are able to ascertain that the floor was left one meter underwater as a result of earthquakes that struck in the 15th century. It is also understood that both floors of this two-story structure were decorated with mosaics. Just past the bishop's house is a temple that is known from an inscription next to the gate to have been erected during the reign of Emperor Marcus Aurelius. Only the gate of this temple, of which it is unknown which god or goddess it was built to honor, survives to this day. This temple, with its 'in antis' plan and Ionic order, lies in a heap of rubble. Let's move away from the trees that blanket the ruins back over to the

Ruins of the baths along the banks of the river that splits Olympos into two.

main avenue of Olympos. This wide avenue runs parallel to the stream. As was previously mentioned, there used to be a bridge to get from one side to the other. One can still see the footprints where the bridge once stood.

On the south side of the stream, opposite the spot where the bridge once spanned, are the remains of the city bath that once had windows. To get to this side of Olympos, you can cross the stream by stepping over some wide stones. It is here that one encounters the theater of Olympos, access of which is not easy as one has to hike through a lot of bushes. The theater's vaulted galleries as well as pieces of decorated doors and niches that are spread over the surrounding area and piled up in the orchestra show this to have been a theater of the classical Roman type. A large Byzantine basilica that lies between the theater and the sea, together with the bath on the banks of the stream

The Sarcophagus of Captain Eudemos which is found in the tomb chamber under the acropolis.

with the wall all make up a fabulous view. In the field between these structures and the stream lies ruins of another structure, which is surrounded on three sides with columns. According to the wide space that is formed in the middle, this site was the city's agora and gymnasium. In moving from the theater towards the west, one can see remnants of a two-story structure on the other side of the stream that dates to the Byzantine period. After a ramp which was constructed of polygonal stone, one encounters the city's necropolis on the hill to the west. Despite the fact that various types of tombs can be seen near the city, tombs located at higher elevations are all of the same type. There are inscriptions on the marble door lintels of the vaulted tombs.

Now, while we are at the spot of the mythological story of the burning stone, which is located an hour outside of Olympos, let's tell the story.

Once upon a time, in Argos Greece, there lived a young man named Bellerophontes who possessed the looks of a god. As he wanted very much to possess the flying horse Pegasus and ran after Pegasus for days over mountains and meadows but couldn't succeed. One day, the gods told him in his dream how he might possess the flying horse. He does what the gods tell him to do and slips the horse a golden bit just as it is drinking water, whereas in this way he is successful. However, one day, Bellerophontes accidentally kills somebody. For this reason, he is forced to leave Argos and take refuge in the palace of the King of Tiryns, Priotos. Not much time passes before the Queen falls in love with the handsome youth, whereas she wants to make love with him. However, as a guest, Bellerophontes does not desire to be disrespectful to the landlord and therefore rejects the queen's desire. The queen gets her revenge by lying to her husband in telling him that the youth tried to force himself upon her. Though the king gets mighty upset, he does not want

172

to kill him, so he sends Bellerophontes to his father-in-law in Lycia with a letter stating that he must be killed.

Bellerophontes reaches Lycia. The king welcomes him near the Xanthos River and puts him up for nine days. On the ninth day, he takes the letter written by his son-in-law and understands that the young man needs to be killed. However, he cannot bring himself to having the young man killed, but instead, wants him to kill the Chimera, thinking that he would be freed of the youth forever.

The Chimera is this strange beast that breathes flames from its mouth, with a front of a lion, the rear of a snake and a middle section of a goat. Bellerophontes carries out the gods' request and thanks to Pegasus, lays the Chimera on the ground. Though the king might had given Bellerophontes a few more tough jobs, he manages to take care of them in fine fashion. As a consequence, the king believes that the youth has something godlike about him, whereby he gives the youth several gifts and gets him to marry his daughter. Bellerophontes comes from the Poseidon lineage. Three children result in this marriage, whereas the daughter Laodameia makes love with Zeus and subsequently gives birth to Sarpedon. Sarpedon grows up to become the Lycian king. He also joins in the Trojan Wars.

In saying "I came a long way from here to help

I came from distant Lycia and the eddying Xanthos,"

He scolds those reluctant to fight and after exhibiting several heroic feats, is killed by Patroclos, who was fighting with the weapons of Achilles. He dies as he turns over his command to Glaucus, while breathing his final breath. Zeus orders Apollo to take his dead son's body to Lycia.

Well, Chimera, who was born as a result of two underground creatures called Typhon and Echidna, lived on a mountain which is visible from Olympos, called Çıralı (Yanartaş). Chimera, which was killed when Bellerophontes rode the flying horse Pegasus, was breathing fire even as it was taking its last breath. The natural gas that spurts out of the ground at regular intervals gets intertwined with this legend. We are going to qualify this flame, not as Chimera's still-burning fire, but one that signifies Lycia's freedom.

A "Burning-Stone" which burns off natural gas. It is accepted that these flames spewed from the mouth of the Chimera monster.

Phaselis

An aerial view of the greenery of Phaselis.

On the way to Antalya, along the newly-opened coastal highway, which allows the most optimum view of the beauties of the Mediterranean, a signpost some 35 kilometers before Antalya leads us along a forest road to Phaselis.

Although the nearby Beldibi Cave shows some signs of prehistoric dwellings, we can trace the city of Phaselis no further back than the 7th century B.C. As it possessed three natural harbors and was close to a rich forested region, Phaselis was founded as a colony of Rhodes in 690 B.C. However, as in the other areas along the Anatolian coastline, there were settlements here before the arrival of colonists from Rhodes, and therefore it was probably founded first by force, or perhaps by gradual integration with the local people,

after their initial acceptance of the colonists.

Phaselis, which derived its existence from the sea in the 6th and 7th centuries, was captured by Persia after they took Anatolia, and later by Alexander the Great after his defeat over Persia. It was here that Alexander accepted many of the envoys from the cities of Pamphylia, then advanced to Gordion, taking each of the coastal cities one after another.

After the death of Alexander, the city remained in Egyptian hands from 209 - 197 B.C. under the reign of the Ptolemies. With the conclusion of the Apemaia Treaty, it was handed over to the Kingdom of Rhodes, together with the other cities of Lycia. From 190 - 160 B.C., it was absorbed into the Lycian League under Roman rule. Like Olympos, Phaselis was under the constant threat of pirates in the 1st century B.C., and the city was even taken over by the pirate Zenicetes for a period, but was freed from the threat when he was defeated by the Romans. In 42 B.C. Brutus had the city linked to Rome. During the Byzantine period, the city became a bishopric. In the 3rd century A.D., its convenient harbor had fallen under the threat of pirates once again and it began to lose importance, suffering further losses at the hands of Arab vessels until becoming totally impoverished in the 11th century.

When the Seljuks began to concentrate on Alanya and Antalya as their ports, Phaselis ceased to be a port of any note.

Phaselis is a city of natural harbors, of which it has no less than three, as we had indicated.

Near the car park is the northern harbor, next to this is the naval base, and to the south is the southern harbor.

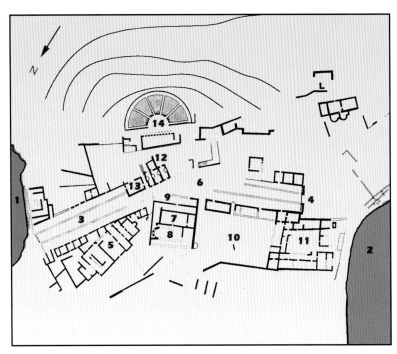

Phaselis Aqueduct.

When the two small islets in the northern harbor were joined to the mainland by a breakwater, the harbor was enlarged and shaped to accommodate a large number of ships. The military harbor to the south of this was protected by a breakwater which extended from the walls around the promontory. It is still possible to see the remains of this breakwater and the walls. Let us look at the other remains to be found in this once-favored port of ancient times, situated at the unsurpassable point between sea and forest that made it one of the gems of antiquity.

As we begin to look over the city of Phaselis, founded over a peninsula that narrowed into bays to the north and south, we first see the ruins of an aqueduct. While water needs were met during Phaselis' early period with cisterns and wells, this basic need was later met with an aqueduct that brought water from faraway places, just like everywhere else in the Roman Empire. Water was brought by aqueduct from a spring to the north of the city to a hill behind the Hadrian Agora where it was distributed within the town through channels and water pipes.

The actual ruins of the city lie on both sides of the main avenue that connects the military harbor with the south harbor. The avenue, which measures 125 meters long by 20-25 meters wide, has sidewalks on either side that are reached by climbing three

steps. After encountering a square in the middle of the avenue, one reaches the south harbor. This avenue, which was laid with flat stones, also had a sewage and drainage system running under it.

Now, by entering this main avenue from the military harbor, one comes across ruins on both sides. The rubble that is seen on the west side were shop lined up along the avenue. Behind these, one encounters a structure with a confusing plan, whereas one sees the bath-gymnasium complex on the other side of this. Behind these were training rooms. Because the gymnasium, which had mosaics on the floor, was used for different reasons in later ages, it lost its original layout. One entered the bath dressing room through two doors in the south, whereas one stepped into the cold and warm sections from here. The floor and walls of the baths, which were constructed in the 3rd century A.D., were once covered in marble, whereas we gather that it was renovated later on and put into use.

The large structure to the south of the bath is an agora. The layout of the agora, which had a wide gate that opened up to the town square, was almost square-shaped and because it was constructed during the reign of Hadrian (117-138 A.D.) it is called Hadrian's Agora. The agora was surrounded by porticos and shops were situated behind the porticos. A basilica with a rectangular layout was added in the

Ruins of the structures lining the main avenue that runs through Phaselis.

177

The Roman Amphitheater of Phaselis.

5th and 6th centuries to the northwest half of Hadrian's Agora, whereas the three-windowed apse can still be seen today. In addition to this, several wings were added to the agora's east and south sides. The large cistern found here is rather interesting.

It is understood that statues once lined the agora's wall edges that overlooked the avenue. It is known that there were two statues at both sides of the entry gate, one of Opramoas, from Rhodiapolis, who helped a number of Lycian cities and who had provided Phaselis with major assistance during this time, as well as that of Saxa Amyntianus. In addition to these statues, there was also a fountain that decorated the facade of the agora.

In making a wide angle, the second section of the avenue begins after the square. One immediately encounters the Domitian Agora at the corner. The building had two gates that faced the avenue. It is called the Domitian Agora due to the fact that an inscription which was written in honor of Emperor Domitian (81-96 A.D.) was found above one of the doors. The courtyard of this agora was in the shape of a major structure complex. Ruins of a final agora on the west side of the avenue belong to a later period. The agora's inner courtyard was surrounded with corridors in a portico manner, and the shops were located in the rear. This agora was connected with the south harbor.

At the end of the main avenue lies Hadrian's Gate. It is possible to see the south harbor with all its magnificence from this gate. The view of a myriad shades of blue sea with mountains in the background topped with winter snow and fog gives the place a mysterious air. Let's take a look at the ruins on the east side by returning back to the main avenue.

Below the theater, one comes across the remnants of another bath. The formation of this bath, which belongs to the 3rd and 4th centuries, was made up of three main spaces that ran parallel to each other. The first space, which once held the swimming pool was known as the frigidarium, the second section was the tepidarium, whereas the third part was the caldarium. Today, the brick foundations that provided heat for the bath can still be seen. To the south of the bath, one may encounter ruins of the town's mosaic-covered public toilet, which was situated on the avenue.

Above this bath, one comes across a theater that once held 1,500-2,000 people. This Hellenistic theater was established on a hill overlooking the town, with a view of the sea, as well. One climbs stone steps to reach the theater from the avenue. The entrance and exit were located on either side. These sections underwent major change during the Byzantine Age. The cavea, which was in the shape of a semi-circle, had 20 rows of seats. The seating areas were divided into five sections by four sets of stairs. The stage originally had two stories, but only the bottom one remains intact. The stage had five doors. The theater continued to be utilized during the Roman period after some changes were made to it. Located on the acropolis in the Temple of Athena above the upper part of the theater was Achilles' broken spear made from ash wood. Ancient writers wrote that while Alexander was in Phaselis, he visited the temple and touched the spear. In addition to the Temple of Athena, we know that there were the temples of Heracles, Hestia and Hermes on the acropolis, which goes back to early period. In addition, there were also palace and official buildings on this site. Today, late-period ruins and cisterns can be seen through a thick blanket of vegetation. Phaselis' necropolis is located in several places. The most widespread one is located along the coastline at the edge of the north harbor. Various types of tombs can be seen here.

A modern yacht has dropped anchor in the ancient harbor of Phaselis.

179

- **TURKEY (ABRIDGED FORMAT)**
  (In English, German and French)
- **TOURISTIC GUIDE OF TURKEY**
  (In English, French, German, Japanese and Turkish)
- **TREASURES OF TURKEY (UNABRIDGED FORMAT)**
  (In English, French, German, Italian and Spanish)
- **THE CITY OF TWO CONTINENTS, ISTANBUL**
  (In English, French, German, Italian and Spanish)
- **TREASURES OF ISTANBUL (UNABRIDGED FORMAT)**
  (In English, French and German)
- **THE TOPKAPI PALACE (ABRIDGED FORMAT)**
  (In English, French, German, Italian, Spanish and Japanese)
- **THE TOPKAPI PALACE (UNABRIDGED FORMAT)**
  (In English, French and German)
- **PAMUKKALE - HIERAPOLIS**
  (In English, French, German, Italian, Spanish, Swedish and Dutch)
- **CAPPADOCIA**
  (In English, French, German, Italian and Spanish)
- **EPHESUS**
  (In English, French and German)
- **MARMARIS - BODRUM**
  (In English, French and German)
- **GUIDE TO EASTERN TURKEY**
  (In English, French and German)
- **ANTALYA**
  (In English, French, German and Italian)
- **MEVLANA AND THE MEVLANA MUSEUM**
  (In English, French and German)
  CHORA
  (In English, French and German)
- **TURKISH CARPET ART**
  (In English, French, German)
- **THE BLUE SAILING (UNABRIDGED FORMAT)**
  (In English)
- **ISTANBUL (ABRIDGED FORMAT)**
  (In English, French and German)
- **ATATÜRK (UNABRIDGED FORMAT)**
  (In English and Turkish)
- **LYCIA**
  (Turkish, In English, French and German)

İLHAN AKŞİT

İlhan Akşit was born in Denizli, Turkey in 1940. He graduated from the Archaeology Department of the Language, History and Geography Faculty in Ankara, in 1965. The following year, he was assigned to a post related to the excavation of Aphrodisias. He was the Director of the Troy Museum in Çanakkale between 1968-1976, during which the replica of the Trojan Horse that we now see on the site was constructed. He also directed the excavation of the Chryse Apollo Temple, in Çanakkale over a period of five years. From 1976-1978, Akşit was appointed as Director of the Underwater Archaeology Museum, in Bodrum and was appointed Director of National Palaces in 1978. During his tenure, the author was responsible for the restoration and reopening of these palaces to the public after an extended period of closure. In 1982, he retired from his post to take up a career as the author of popular books on Turkish archaeology and tourism. To date, he has nearly 30 titles to his credit, including 'The Story of Troy', 'Anatolian Civilizations', 'The Blue Journey', 'Istanbul', 'The Hittites', 'Cappadocia', 'Topkapı Palace', 'Pamukkale', 'Antalya', 'Ephesus', 'Turkey', 'Mustafa Kemal Atatürk' and 'Lycia, the Illuminated Nation'.